ArtScroll Series®

Rabbi Nosson Scherman / Rabbi Meir Zlotowitz

General Editors

Dear Son

Published by
Mesorah Publications, ltd

*A father's wise
guidance for
wholesome human
relationships,
a happy
marriage and
a serene home*

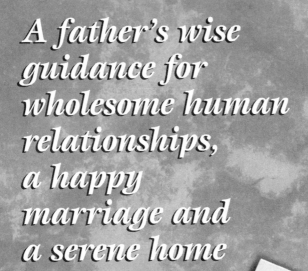

by
**Rabbi Eliyohu
Goldschmidt**

FIRST EDITION
First Impression … October 2004

Published and Distributed by
MESORAH PUBLICATIONS, LTD.
4401 Second Avenue / Brooklyn, N.Y 11232

Distributed in Europe by
LEHMANNS
Unit E, Viking Business Park
Rolling Mill Road
Jarow, Tyne & Wear, NE32 3DP
England

Distributed in Australia and New Zealand by
GOLDS WORLDS OF JUDAICA
3-13 William Street
Balaclava, Melbourne 3183
Victoria, Australia

Distributed in Israel by
SIFRIATI / A. GITLER — BOOKS
6 Hayarkon Street
Bnei Brak 51127

Distributed in South Africa by
KOLLEL BOOKSHOP
Shop 8A Norwood Hypermarket
Norwood 2196, Johannesburg, South Africa

Typography by CompuScribe at ArtScroll Studios, Ltd.

Printed in the United States of America by Noble Book Press Corp.
Bound by Sefercraft, Quality Bookbinders, Ltd., Brooklyn N.Y. 11232

This volume is dedicated

לעילוי נשמת

The Author

Rabbi Boruch Eliyohu זצ״ל Goldschmidt

הרב ברוך אליהו בן החבר יחזקאל זצ״ל גולדשמיט

נפטר כ״ו אב תש״ס

משגיח רוחני, ישיבה זכרון משה סאוט פאלסבורג

יהי זכרו ברוך

תנצב״ה

Table of Contents

Biography

A Baal Mussar's Legacy

Rav Eliyohu Goldschmidt *z.tz.l.* was a quiet *gadol*. He kept a low profile. He did not attend conventions and conferences. He was not involved in political or broad communal issues. He learned in the Lakewood Yeshivah for many years, and then was *mashgiach* of the South Fallsburg Yeshivah for the rest of his life. His life was Torah, Mussar and *tefillah*, and he spent his time in the *koslei beis midrash*, virtually day and night, deeply absorbed in his learning and in caring for his *talmidim* and setting them firmly on the path of righteousness. Over that period of time, he had a profound influence on thousands of young men, many of whom went on to become *roshei yeshivah, maggidei shiur* and rabbis, the future leaders of *Klal Yisrael*.

The Early Years

Reb Eliyohu's parents, Yechezkel and Sarah Goldschmidt, were German Jews. Yechezkel was born in Hochstadt, a tiny village 15 minutes by horse-and-buggy from Frankfurt-am-Main. The entire Jewish community of Hochstadt consisted of no more than seven families, but it was staunchly Orthodox and had it own little shul.

Yechezkel was sent away to school in Frankfurt, where he boarded with an uncle and attended the Rabbiner Samson Raphael Hirsch School. At the age of 17, he went to work as a salesman for a metal company. After he married, he and his wife settled in Hochstadt, where they opened a hardware store. Yechezkel was hardworking, meticulous and scrupulously honest, and he provided a decent living for his family. Their first child, Yosef, was born in 1933. Eliyohu was born in 1935 and their third son, Aharon Shlomo, was born in 1945, long after they had left Germany.

As the situation for the Jewish people in Germany deteriorated during the 1930s, the Goldschmidts, among many others, seriously considered leaving the country. They left Germany by ship, in 1938, a few months before Kristallnacht, and arrived in Buenos Aires, Argentina with a group of other refugees on Yom Kippur.

At that time, there were very few observant Jews in Buenos Aires, and religious education for the children was almost nonexistent. Yechezkel found an apartment in a non-Jewish neighborhood and opened a textile importing business.

In 1940, the Goldschmidts moved to Belgrano, a more Jewish neighborhood, and given Yechezkel's experience in metals, he opened a steel company. He joined the Achdus Yisrael shul and became close with its rabbi, Rabbi Shlomo Klein. He became active in the community, serving as president of the shul and coordinator of the building committee. He also arranged the *shiurim*, made sure that everything was there for *shalosh seudos* and helped with the *shechitah*. Despite his prominent position in the shul, however, he never sat at the *mizrach* wall. Instead, he chose to sit right next to the *bimah* so that he could hear the *kriah* better.

Yechezkel was a devoted reader and follower of Rav Samson Raphael Hirsch's works. During these years, he undertook to write a Hirsch commentary in Spanish, and he invested a great deal of time and effort in the project. His purpose was purely for the good of the community, and when he heard that someone else was working on a similar project, he readily gave it up.

Because there was no yeshivah in Buenos Aires, the Goldschmidt boys were sent to the Testalozzi Elementary School, a public school. Three times a week they attended Talmud Torah in the afternoons for two hours, where they studied with R' Isser Masel and afterward with R' Nissim Pecker. That was the extent of their formal Torah education.

The Goldschmidts were a strictly observant family, which was somewhat of a rarity in Buenos Aires in those days, even in the Orthodox community. It was not easy for Eliyohu to grow up observant when most of his friends were not. It was not easy wearing a *yarmulke* to public school when no one else did. It was not easy being restricted from going to some of the places his friends frequented. It was not easy having to stay home Shabbos and Yom Tov when his friends were out having a good time.

As he wrote in his book *Dear Daughter:* "When I was growing up, a family such as mine, that adhered to Torah and *mitzvos*, was a rarity. Because of my family's observance, I faced far more restrictions and deprivations than my friends did. We did have kosher meat and one kind of kosher cheese, but beyond that, there were absolutely no kosher products available.

"What natural reaction would you expect from a boy in my situation? Resentment? Jealousy? Well, let me tell you, I felt nothing of the sort. It simply did not occur to me to envy my friends who came from more permissive families. My parents had created a home that was an island of holiness, a fortress to defend our family against the world around us. Our home was a happy, secure place, a veritable Gan Eden."

Another factor also insulated him against his environment. It was, as he writes in *Dear Daughter*, the wonderful *shalom bayis* between his mother and father that reigned in his home. He saw his home as an island of bliss, a haven of peace and tranquility that was so appealing to him that everything his parents did and asked of him was more desirable than anything he saw elsewhere.

When Eliyohu was 6 years old, the family went to a summer colony, and he got his little finger stuck in a door. His fingertip was nearly severed, remaining attached to the finger only by a sliver of skin. Through the resourcefulness of an aunt, he received immediate medical attention, and the severed tip was reattached. It was an exceedingly painful and traumatic experience for young Eliyohu, but he was deeply appreciative of all that was done for him. Right then and there, he decided to become a doctor so that he could help other people, just as he himself had been helped. Ultimately, this concern for other people would express itself in different ways, but the sentiments were already there at an early age.

The sweet voice was also there at a young age. Eliyohu's voice was extraordinarily beautiful and he was in demand to sing solos at occasions such as weddings and *sheva berachos*. He was also part of the shul choir until his bar mitzvah, when his voice changed. He was also invited to sing in the opera, but his father adamantly refused to permit this. Ultimately, he would use his voice to *daven* Shacharis before the *amud* on Rosh Hashanah and Yom Kippur and to inspire thousands of *bnei yeshivah* over the years.

By the time he was bar mitzvah, Eliyohu's Torah learning was limited to Chumash and Rashi. One day, a man asked him if he had ever learned Mishnayos. He had not. The man opened a *Mishnah Bava Kamma* to the first mishnah in the third *perek* and asked Eliyohu to read it. With difficulty, and a little help, he managed to read and translate the mishnah. This, his first venture into the Talmud, sparked his interest in broadening his knowledge and also awakened a keen taste for *chiddush*, the facility for analysis and original interpretation.

Eliyohu completed high school in 1953 and enrolled in medical school. One year, he decided to spend his summer vacation in *Eretz Yisrael.* Since the summers in Argentina correspond to the winter months in the Northern Hemisphere, he arrived in *Eretz Yisrael* in the middle of the school year. He joined Yeshivah Kol Torah, where he learned Mussar and became very close with Rav Gedaliah Eiseman, the *mashgiach.* He also got to know the *rosh yeshivah,* Rav Shlomo Zalman Auerbach, who made a very deep impression on him. In particular, he could not get over Rav Shlomo Zalman's aura of absolute serenity. He was a man who seemed to have everything his heart desired, a man completely at peace with himself. And what did he have? The four *amos* of Halachah. Nothing else mattered.

The Argentine summer vacation drew to a close. It was time for Eliyohu to return to medical school, but his brief stay in the yeshivah had transformed him. He wrote to his parents that he wanted to stay on, but they insisted that he return home and earn his medical degree. Eliyohu complied. Back in Argentina, he returned to medical school, while continuing to learn informally on his own with various study partners. He also taught in the Talmud Torah during the afternoons. In medical school, he excelled in his studies and showed promise of becoming a great doctor.

In 1958, Rabbi Zaidel Semiaticki, a distinguished former *talmid* of the Mirrer Yeshivah, arrived in Buenos Aires, hoping to found a yeshivah, but he passed away only several months after his arrival. At the funeral, Eliyohu was so moved that right then and there he decided to leave medical school and go to learn in a yeshivah. On a *pushka* he found the address of Beth Medrash Govoha in Lakewood, and wrote a letter to the office asking them to send him a student visa. Although this was an unusual request to come out of the blue from Argentina, the visa arrived in a very short time. Eliyohu took this as a clear sign that this is what he was meant to do.

In 1959, he arrived in Lakewood. He walked into the *beis midrash*, took one look at the face of Rav Aharon Kotler, the *rosh yeshivah,* and knew he had made the right decision. This was where he belonged.

The Middle Years

Rav Aharon Kotler, the great *gaon* and *tzaddik*, the *gadol hador*, took an instant liking to the young Eliyohu Goldschmidt. In him Rav Aharon perceived true sincerity, a pure heart, a passion to learn, and sparks of greatness. Although Eliyohu was still at a very unsophisticated level of learning, and Rav Aharon's *shiurim* were wonders of dazzling genius, Rav Aharon told him to come to the *shiurim* right away. He was confident that his progress would be quick and dramatic. And indeed it was. Unknown to Eliyohu, Rav Aharon would often speak proudly of the former medical student who had come to Lakewood with an unquenchable thirst for Torah and had become a shining *talmid*.

When Eliyohu was 25, he became engaged to Michelle Lehmann of Montivideo. Her uncle and Eliyohu's father had been classmates in Germany. The families shared the same values, as did their children. Rav Aharon suggested that Eliyohu learn for two years before the marriage. These would be excellent years, because he would be free of concerns about getting married and also free of the *reichaim al tzavoro*, the inevitable distractions of a growing family.

Eliyohu was concerned, however, that his *kallah* would not agree to it. "She will agree," said Rav Aharon, and indeed she did, as if it were the most natural request in the world. Mrs. Goldschmidt was concerned, however, about how they would support themselves in the *kollel*. Reb Eliyohu reassured her, saying, "Just as Hashem helps the forty other families in the *kollel*, He will help the forty-first."

One year after the engagement, Rav Aharon told Eliyohu that he could get married without waiting any longer. The Goldschmidts settled down to a blissful life in the small *kollel* of Lakewood. They counted the pennies and lived modestly, especially as the family grew with periodic new additions, but they were happy and content. The joy of learning never left the two of them. Their happiness at being privileged to be part of the *kollel* community radiated to everyone who knew them.

During these years, Eliyohu set himself on the path he would follow for the rest of his life. With tremendous *hasmadah*, he spent almost all his waking time in the *beis midrash*, learning with unflagging drive and passion. He progressed quickly in his learning. He also progressed in his *avodah* and *tefillah*. He learned Mussar diligently and was a living example of the ideals portrayed in the Mussar works. He was kind and considerate to everyone with whom he came into contact, and he carefully weighed and measured every word that came out of his mouth. He became one of the recognized *talmidei chachamim* of Lakewood, outstanding not only in his *lomdus* but also in his *tzidkus*.

The Goldschmidts raised their eight children in a simple three-bedroom apartment. There were guests every Shabbos and often during the week. Space may have been at a premium, but there was warmth in abundance, and the children never felt deprived. The boys and girls who grew up in that home all have contented families of their own, a tribute to the legacy of their parents, who showed them by example how to live simply but happily, and to find fulfillment in a life of Torah.

Shortly after Eliyohu's marriage, Rav Aharon invited him to be the *baal tefillah* for Shacharis on Rosh Hashanah and Yom Kippur. His personal qualities certainly qualified him for the honor, and his beautiful, sweet, and emotion-filled voice inspired the *talmidim* of the yeshivah to reach the high levels of devotion and concentration called for on the holiest days of the year.

In 1965, Rav Schneur Kotler, who had succeeded his late father as *rosh yeshivah,* asked Rav Eliyohu to deliver *vaadim* (guided Mussar discussion groups) for Torah Vodaath *talmidim* who had come to spend their summer vacation in the Lakewood Yeshivah. The *vaadim* were so successful that he was asked to continue them all year round. Every Friday night, he would say *vaadim* for three different groups. Some of the young men who attended his inspirational talks were among the finest *talmidim* in the yeshivah. As a measure of Reb Eliyohu's great humility, he asked Rav Eliezer Shach if it was appropriate for him to say a *vaad* to people who were greater in Torah than he. Rav Shach reassured him that it was perfectly fine and that he need not be concerned. So magnetic was his personality and so wise his presentations that there were times when he led the amazing total of twenty-one *vaadim* a week — and all the while he maintained his regular three *sedarim* a day.

One thing led to another. His *vaadim* were so full of insight into the human mind and heart that people began to come to him for advice on personal matters, especially regarding *shalom bayis,* issues of marital relationships. He approached such questions with an open mind, analyzing the situations and the motivations behind them. Invariably, his advice was rooted in a Gemara, a Midrash, a Rambam, a Rabbeinu Yonah, a Ramban or some other source in the Torah and its commentaries. The results were so excellent that he was invited to give a regular *vaad* on *shalom bayis* to young married men, in addition to his other *vaadim*. From then on, he became one of the most important sources of Torah advice on *shalom bayis*, serving not only the people living in Lakewood, but many others who came or wrote to him from far beyond.

The Later Years

In 1980, Reb Eliyohu was invited to become the *mashgiach* of the South Fallsburg Yeshivah in the Catskill Mountains, a 4-hour bus ride from Lakewood. Because he did not want to move his family from Lakewood, he was given a room in the dormitory — with a private bathroom, a bookcase and the bare necessities. There he lived during the week, going home for Shabbos and Yom Tov. That room became his home away from home for the rest of his life.

One can only imagine how difficult this must have been for Rebbetzin Goldshmidt — the loneliness and the increased burden of raising the family. But the idealism she demonstrated all her life came to the fore now, as well. She encouraged him and, as always, stood by his side.

At first, Reb Eliyohu would travel to South Fallsburg early Sunday morning and return to Lakewood late Monday evening. Then he would return to South Fallsburg Wednesday morning and come back to Lakewood for Shabbos. During his days in the yeshivah, he would call home every morning at 7 o'clock and review the homework with the children. Eventually, when it became too difficult and disruptive for him to return home in the middle of the week, he spent the entire week in the yeshivah, living like a *yeshivah bachur*.

Although his official position in the yeshivah was *mashgiach*, he learned in the *beis midrash* all three *sedarim* with a *chavrusa* like any other *bachur*, and he was always on time. Furthermore, he was always in the *beis midrash* before Shacharis so that he could prepare himself properly; no one remembers ever having seen him come even a minute late. He prepared every *vaad* and *shmuess* on his own time and not during the *sedarim* of the yeshivah.

More amazing, he also attended religiously the *shiurim* of the *rosh yeshivah*, Rav Elya Ber Wachtfogel, and hung on every word. Afterward, he would discuss the *shiur* with the *bachurim*, and he did not hesitate to go to the *rosh yeshivah* for clarification, if necessary. Part of his motivation for attending the *shiurim* was undoubtedly to show respect, but it was much more than that. Rav Eliyohu loved learning above all else, and he was genuinely interested in hearing the *chiddushim* of the *rosh yeshivah*. He would also circulate around the *beis midrash* like any other *talmid*, in order to hear good *kushios* or *sevaros* that others had to offer.

Once Reb Eliyohu had to go to the wedding of a *talmid* in Montreal, which was seven hours away by car. He asked the *bachurim* with whom he would be traveling if they would mind learning in the car on the road. They agreed and brought Gemaras; the yeshivah was learning *Gittin* at the time. They probably expected that some time during the trip they would discuss a topic in the Gemara. But that is not what happened. As soon as they got on the road, Reb Eliyohu opened his Gemara to *daf* 13, the *sugya* of *maamad shelashtan*. He explained that although the *rosh yeshivah* might not get that far, nevertheless they should make the effort to learn it now. For the entire trip, until the fading light made it difficult to see the Gemara, they learned as if they were in the *beis midrash*. Reb Eliyohu could not tolerate wasting time that could be spent learning.

Perhaps most important of all, the *talmidim* in the yeshivah had the privilege of seeing and learning from the way he conducted himself all day every day: his love of learning, his *hasmadah*, his *yiras shamayim*, his passionate *tefillah*, his sterling *middos*, even the way he ate. Most of the time, he would take his meals in the privacy of his room, but on Motza'ei Yom Kippur he ate in the dining room together with the *bachurim*. One of them recalls that between every bite he would lay his fork on the table. As long as he was still chewing the food, his mind was on other things. He said that people should come away from a Yom Kippur with some patience.

Despite Reb Eliyohu's complete absorption in his learning, he was nonetheless always aware of every *bachur* in the yeshivah and sensitive to his needs. If a new *bachur* had trouble adjusting, he would sense it and help him over the hurdles. If a *bachur* was not feeling the full enjoyment of his learning, he would find ways of sparking his excitement. If he saw a *bachur* with the slightest frown on his face, he would call him aside and ask if everything was all right.

This is how he dealt not only with the *talmidim* but also with any person he encountered. Always with a warm smile. Always with a caring heart. Always with absolute honesty and integrity. Once, as a favor to a friend, he went to pick up an airline ticket from a travel agent When the agent gave him the ticket, Reb Eliyohu thanked him warmly and profusely, as if the ticket had been for him.

His scrupulous honesty was truly a marvel. He once sent his daughter to summer camp, and, because he lived on a limited income, he negotiated a reduced price and extended payment schedule with the camp. His payments arrived regularly as arranged. At the end of the summer, however, the payments were added up, and it turned out that he had overpaid quite substantially. The camp sent him a refund, but he declined to accept it. "After we negotiated the price," he explained, "there was an improvement in my income. The price we had agreed on was based on my earlier situation. Since my situation improved, I should pay more."

Reb Eliyohu was very diligent in showing respect, consideration, and gratitude to his parents. He would go to Argentina to visit them every year during the month of Av, when the yeshivah was not in session. In the later years, until his mother passed away in 1991, he would go several times a year. During his visits, his father would often arrange for him to speak in public. He would have preferred not to speak, but he knew that such public appearances would give his parents much satisfaction. On one fourteen-day visit, he spoke fourteen times in various shuls and institutions, while his father listened with quiet pride.

All in all, Reb Eliyohu was a genuine *ehrlicher Yid*, a man who lived every moment of his life according to the instructions and the values of the holy Torah. He was a living *sefer* of Mussar, a shining example for his *talmidim*, his family and everyone else with whom he came into contact.

Joy Through Growth

To Reb Eliyohu, a life without constant growth was not a true life. He would say that a 2-year-old has lovable antics that make people laugh and shower his parents with compliments, but if the child is still carrying on the same way at the age of 20, he is an object of pity. Life cannot be stagnant; a person must grow.

And the way to do that is to look for new challenges. During his nineteen years in South Fallsburg, he never repeated a Mussar lecture, thus exerting a constant pressure on himself to think, learn, and originate — and consequently to grow. But the pressure never caused him to be tense or depressed. Once, speaking to Reb Shneur, he quoted a *Kli Yakar* which says that one who learns without worries will remember his learning. And he exclaimed, "Rebbi, I have no worries!"

Positive thinking was of his essence. Many a conscientious *bachur* expresses remorse that he didn't learn enough during the just ended yeshivah year. Reb Eliyohu would respond, "First concentrate on how much you *did* learn. When you are happy with what you have accomplished, you will work harder to accomplish even more. He would say that anyone who learns Mussar and becomes depressed at his inadequacies simply does not understand the essence of Mussar.

His joy at the privilege of performing a *mitzvah* was extraordinary. He would wake up early on Succos to perform the *mitzvah* of *Dalet Minnim*, and when he shook his *lulav*, he would literally dance and his face would shine. As the Midrash teaches, the *lulav* symbolizes the Jew's successful emergence from the judgment of Yom Kippur. What could be a greater cause for joy!

Time was a precious commodity because it was a gift that, if squandered, could not be recouped. On Thursday nights in South Fallsburg, when he had to leave before the end of the Mussar *seder* to catch the last bus to New York, he would have his bag packed and leave it at the door. A taxi would be ordered to come at the last possible moment, and he would leave after the first 4 minutes of the Mussar *seder*. Why wait until then? And how much could be gained from only 4 minutes? Such questions never entered his mind. Even a minute was precious — and 4 minutes were a priceless treasure.

The Hand of Hashem

To him, Hashem's providence was not an abstract concept; he felt it in everything he did. "Why should you be nervous about what will be? If Hashem took care of you till now, why would He stop?"

In one of his notebooks, he had a list of things for which to be grateful. Among them, he listed having glasses to enable him to see clearly, and being spared from the pain of a toothache. Life was filled with goodness; one had only to recognize it.

Someone told him about a wedding where there was a fire scare in the kitchen and the fire department responded to the alarm. So loud was the music that the revelers did not hear the alarm and they thought that the firefighters were dancers in disguise. Reb Eliyohu likened this to the shofar blasts of Elul. Instead of hearing and recognizing them as a call to repent, they are drowned out by the "music" of the pleasure and distractions of this world.

To him, even his success in helping people with their *shalom bayis* had nothing to do with his personal ability. He would attribute everything to Hashem's helping hand.

Middos and Mitzvos

He greeted everyone with a smile and, busy though he was, he had time for everyone, saying, "For you I have all the time you need." When he took part in the wedding or *bris* of a *talmid,* it was his *simchah,* and his smile showed it.

He once had to speak to a younger *rosh yeshivah* in *Eretz Yisrael* about a *bachur.* The *rosh yeshivah* had once learned in Lakewood for a short time, and Reb Eliyohu introduced himself saying, "You probably don't remember me." The *rosh yeshivah* answered, "When I came to Lakewood, the first person to welcome me with a warm *Shalom Aleichem* was you. I will never forget it." That was typical, because he never passed up an opportunity to offer friendship or help.

Part of his consideration for others was to tailor his *vaad* or personal talks according to the needs of the listener, never merely to mouth standard platitudes. When he came from South Fallsburg to Lakewood for Shabbos, he gave three *vaadim* on Friday night, and each one was different, according to the needs of the participants. Part of his dedication to others was to step back if he felt that others could be more effective than he. When Rabbi Mattisyahu Salomon became the *mashgiach* in Lakewood, Reb Eliyohu asked him to deliver a regular *shmuess* on *Yom Kippur Kattan* (the day before Rosh Chodesh). Reb Mattisyahu did not learn until years later that Reb Eliyohu had canceled his own regular *vaad* so that the *talmidim* would be able to attend Reb Mattisyahu's *shmuess.*

During the Gulf War, he would rise early and recite *Tehillim* with bitter tears, praying for the safety and peace of mind of Israelis threatened by Scud rockets. In his Machzor and Siddur were the names of people whom he kept in mind during his *tefillos.*

Before the *Yamim Noraim,* he would ask a *bachur* to prepare a list of all the *talmidim* and their mothers' name, so that he could have them in mind during his *tefillos.*

When he *davened,* he felt that he was actually speaking to Hashem, and Hashem was listening to every word. And since that was so, he would never rush through his prayers, no matter where he was or how hectic the schedule might be. One would never be so discourteous to a human listener, surely one dared not be less courteous to the One Who is listening to his *tefillos.* This was an attitude that he projected to his children and *talmidim.*

The Legacy

Even before he left Lakewood for South Fallsburg, Reb Eliyohu was already renowned as an expert in *shalom bayis* matters. With the advancing years, he gained an ever broadening mastery of the Torah and the concepts of *Chazal.* At the same time, his experience as guide and counselor to innumerable young men seeking to get married or newly married deepened his knowledge and understanding of the Jewish mind, heart and soul. He attained a clear sense of how a Jewish man and woman can join together in a perfect union to create a Gan Eden and a *kiddush Hashem* in their home.

In 1992, at the request of his father that he publish something in memory of his mother who had recently passed away, he wrote *Sefer Seichel Tov.* It is a lofty work of Mussar for *talmidei chachamim,* a view of the words of *Chazal* through the analytic prism of *lomdus.* It was so popular that it was reprinted in 1997, but it did not serve the needs of a broader public, both because of its level of erudition and because it is in Hebrew.

In 1999, Reb Eliyohu yielded to public pressure and published *Dear Daughter* in English, a book of advice written in the format of warm and chatty letters to a daughter. In addition to a solid foundation of quotations from *Chazal,* the commentators and classic Mussar works, *Dear Daughter* is an inexhaustible wellspring of stories and vignettes from his own life and the lives of people he knew. On almost every page, colorful characters come to life and struggle with a range of situations. Through these, the author directs his daughter to discover the pearls of wisdom that will sanctify her home, gladden her heart, and enrich her life.

The book was such a success that it became almost required reading for every girl engaged to be married or seriously considering marriage. It also transformed many homes by infusing them with a new insight into the exquisite bond that unites husband and wife.

But men and women are two entirely different creatures, as the author never ceases to point out, and the advice of a kindly father to his daughter is not identical to the advice he would give his son. Therefore, the public demanded that Reb Eliahu continue his work and write *Dear Son*, in a style and format similar to *Dear Daughter*. Once again, Reb Eliyohu bowed to public pressure and invested a great amount of his precious time into the new manuscript.

On 26 Av, 5760/2000, when the manuscript was almost complete, Reb Eliyohu was suddenly stricken and passed away, at the too-young age of 64. Through the efforts of the family, the manuscript, supplemented by material adapted from *Sefer Seichel Tov*, was completed as he would have wished. *Dear Son*, the book you are holding in your hands, is the result.

Not many people have the *zechus* of leaving such a rich heritage behind them, as did Reb Eliahu Goldschmidt *z.tz.l.* He is survived by a large and beautiful family and thousands of devoted *talmidim*. He also personally touched and inspired the lives of many thousands more. And perhaps most important of all, he brought serenity and joy into the homes of thousands of Jewish families, strengthening the bonds of mutual love and respect between husbands and wives and fostering a harmonious environment in which children could grow up with stability and security and the opportunity to fulfill their promise.

May his memory be a blessing.

Preface

In his role as a *mashgiach* in a major yeshivah, our father *z.tz.l.* dealt with all sorts of *shalom bayis* issues. He also used to give a weekly *vaad* to young married men, providing guidance on the importance of husband and wife being the king and queen of their home in the fullest sense. Eventually, our father wrote for the general public about *shalom bayis* issues. At first, he published *Sefer Seichel Tov* in Hebrew. Years later, he published *Dear Daughter* in English, a book specifically geared for women.

When *Dear Daughter* was published, the response was overwhelming. People called our father day and night with their questions and problems, and despite his busy schedule, he managed to make time to help them as much as he could. At the same time, there was a great demand for a similar book geared for men.

This was not an easy undertaking for him. Most of the year, almost all his time was taken up by his role as *mashgiach* and his dedication to spend three *sedarim* a day learning in the *beis midrash,* despite his other responsibilities. Nonetheless, he tried to make time to write whenever he could. Around the Yamim Tovim and during the few weeks of his summer vacation, he wrote all day. At the time of his sudden passing, he was writing the final chapters of this book. *Baruch Hashem*, after much hard work, we are able to bring his final book to publication, and all the efforts he invested into it have borne fruit.

As our father mentioned in *Dear Daughter*: My purpose in writing was to raise the consciousness of Jewish families about issues that can interfere with the peace and harmony of their homes. This advice was not meant to represent an authoritative final word. I am sure others may have variations about how to achieve the ends which we all seek. Only with regard to the unequivocal prohibition against arguing in the presence of children am I willing to take an authoritative position.

As we worked to prepare our father's manuscript for publication, we were reminded of special moments we shared with him. When our respective times came to begin considering marriage, our father would sit us down for a talk. He explained that a Jewish home is a *mikdash me'at*, a minor *Beis HaMikdash*. Just as in the *Beis HaMikdash* there were many different utensils, each with its own special sanctity and designated place, so is it in a Jewish home. It is not just a place where husband and wife live together. It is a dwelling place for the *Shechinah*, the Divine Presence. And everything in the home should have its special role in creating an atmosphere of Torah and holiness appropriate for such a dwelling place. "Keep this is mind when you are looking for a wife," he would tell us. "Consider carefully if she is the *eizer kenegdo*, the helpmate, who will join you in establishing a *mikdash me'at*."

Our father would tell us, "When you get married, you have a clean slate. You can't excuse the things you do, even though they can be done in a better way, by saying that this is how you always did them. This is a fresh start, an opportunity to make resolutions that will last, to set up your home and institute good practices, such as saying a *dvar Torah*, even a very short one, at every Shabbos meal."

He once explained in a *vaad* one method to lend stability to a marriage. He told the story of our grandmother, who left her home in Germany to settle in Argentina, a land bereft of Yiddishkeit and so different from the home she knew. When asked how she was able to manage, she explained, "The gates of Germany were sealed." She knew there was no way she could return, so she had no choice but to make this, her new home, the best it could be. In marriage, our father explained, it is the same. We have to realize that there is no turning back. When we realize we are in this marriage for good, then we will invest all our strength into making it work.

Our father taught us that the husband and wife are the king and queen of the home. We learned to stand up when either of our parents entered the room, and we always offered them our assistance without being asked. There was a level of awe and respect when we spoke to them, and of course, we would not dare answer back. Our father, with his regular telephone calls and visits to his parents in Argentina, taught by example how to respect parents. "Your children will value what you value," he would tell us. "If you make Torah the most important thing in your life, it will be the most important thing in their lives as well."

Our father taught us how to handle the challenges of life. "Watch a baby learn to walk," he would say. "He falls, and he gets up and tries again. This can happen again and again without the child becoming frustrated. This is the way we should handle the difficulties sent our way. You try your best, again and again, and you will succeed in the end."

He once told us the story of a family that had no money. Every time they needed to make a large purchase which they could not afford, they would call a meeting to discuss whether they should take money from a certain emergency account they had. Each time, they decided that the purchase was not important enough to warrant depleting the emergency fund.

Many years later, when the children were grown, one of them asked his father about the emergency account. "It doesn't exist," his father replied. "I just wanted you to grow up secure that you had everything you needed."

Our father pointed out to us that it is neither money nor any of the material extras that make children feel secure, but rather the feeling that their parents care for them and will supply them with whatever they need.

Our father always gave us everything we needed. And now that he is no longer with us to teach and to guide us, he has left us his legacy — his words of wisdom and his teachings — through the books that he wrote and the lessons that he taught based on the teachings of *Chazal* and his *rebbeim*.

We would like to pay homage to our dear mother, Mrs. Michelle Goldschmidt, who was always the epitome of a true *eizer kenegdo*. She stood by our father all through the years with tremendous *mesiras nefesh* and is an equal partner in all that he became and in everything he accomplished.

We would like to express our deep gratitude to Rabbi Nosson Scherman and Rabbi Meir Zlotowitz of Mesorah Publications, who were committed to enable us to present this book to the broader public. We are indebted to them for all they have done to make this a reality.

A special note of thanks to Rabbi Yaakov Yosef Reinman, who brought the manuscript to its final form with such clarity and grace. Our father was very pleased with Rabbi Reinman's work on *Dear Daughter*, and we are confident he would have been equally appreciative of his efforts on this book.

Rabbi Yisroel Dick, our dear brother-in-law, contributed his time, his wisdom and his sharp analysis during the different stages of the publication process and helped make the dream of this book a reality. Thank you.

A heartfelt thanks to Mrs. Devorah Goldschmidt. This book would have been impossible without the countless hours she spent in front of the computer in the early stages of this volume.

In closing, we offer up our prayer to the *Ribbono Shel Olam* that the publication of this book will increase and enhance *shalom bayis* in Jewish homes all over the world and that this should be a *zechus* for our father's *neshamah* in Gan Eden.

Aaron, Ephraim and Pinchos Goldschmidt
Rosh Chodesh Cheshvan, 5765 (2004)
Lakewood, New Jersey

Introduction
A Garden of Eden

My dear son,

Have you ever wondered what set me on the journey from Buenos Aires, a city barren of Jewish spirituality, to where I am today, having raised a family in Lakewood and seeing all my children becoming *bnei Torah*? It was a little book I came across, a description of the Chafetz Chaim's *yeshivah* in Radun. The author wrote glowingly about the beauty and nobility of *yeshivah* life and, in doing so, he ignited a fire in my heart. I yearned to experience the exquisite spiritual pleasures he described. I was so inspired that I dreamed about joining such a *yeshivah* and, eventually, my dream came true.

One book changed my life. It can happen. Now I want to tell you about another time a relatively minor event changed someone's life. My friend told me this story.

My friend's parents were elderly people who suffered from a variety of ailments. One afternoon, while they were in the elevator in their apartment building, a mechanical problem caused it to jam while they were between floors. Everyone was stranded in the elevator for over an hour, and during all this time, the two elderly people were completely concerned with each other's ailments. Husband and wife disregarded their own aches and pains and did everything in their power to ease the aches and pains of the other. The other people trapped in the elevator marveled at their selfless devotion to each other in an hour of panic and stress.

A few weeks later, my friend's mother received a letter from a woman who had relatives in their building. She knew his mother's name because she visited the building frequently and was familiar with the residents. For quite a while, she wrote, she had been having problems in her marriage. Her husband, she claimed, was selfish and inconsiderate. The situation had deteriorated to the point that she was ready to divorce him. When stranded on the elevator with my friend's parents, however, she had witnessed their outstanding devotion to each other. This impressed her so much that she decided to give her marriage another try, and she was writing to thank my friend's mother for her unwitting help.

Would you have thought that she would react this way when she saw these old people so devoted to each other? Wouldn't you have assumed that her response wold be the exact opposite? Here she sees two people so considerate of each other, while she is suffering with an inconsiderate husband. The example of the old people should have shown her how much she was missing in her marriage and convinced her to cut her husband loose and seek a better source — but, no. This was not her reaction. She decided to salvage her own marriage. Why do you think she felt this way?

It was because her whole concept of marriage was transformed when she saw my friend's parents. Her approach had always been a selfish one, always seeking what she could get out of her marriage, and so she gave very little and was resentful when she received very little from her husband. She decided he was inconsiderate, but when she saw the marvelous marriage that these two elderly people had, she understood that she was missing out on a piece of paradise. She suddenly saw herself and her husband in a different light, and she decided to give their marriage a fresh start.

The Ramban writes that the *berachah* of *Asher Bara*, which blesses the *chassan* and *kallah* with so many different forms of joy and friendship, brings them perception and wisdom. What is the connection between friendship and wisdom? The answer may lie in the *Tomar Devorah's* explanation of the Divine wisdom, as the Creator's ability to care and to provide for even the smallest need of even the most minute creature. This is true wisdom, and between husband and wife it is expressed in the care and devotion they show each other. Their joy and friendship leads to wisdom of the highest order.

Sometimes, however, we lose sight of this wonderful blessing. We become so caught up in the cares and burdens of daily life that the paradise in our home becomes obscured. Then we become distressed, and we are not quite sure why.

A young man once came to me to complain about his situation at home. At first, he spoke in vague generalities, but he became more specific after I pressed him. I let him blow off some steam.

"I don't understand her," he said. "I came home for lunch. She was expecting me, you know. She asked what I wanted to have for lunch, so there was no mistake. She knew I was coming home. So I came home, and she's not there. So I waited. I thought maybe she just had to run out for something. An egg or something. Who knows? So okay, what's a few minutes anyway? It's no big deal. But then it was more than a few minutes. After a half hour, she still wasn't there. I was getting really upset, so I just kept looking at my watch, because I was sure she was coming in any second, you know. But she didn't. She came home after I was waiting for an hour. A whole hour! So what was the emergency? I wanted to know. Did she have to take someone to the hospital or something? It turns out that she got into a conversation with a neighbor, and she just couldn't get away from her. That's what she says, but I don't buy it. What do you mean you can't get away? You tell her that your husband is waiting, and then you say good-bye. I was so angry, I didn't know what to do with myself. And things have been pretty much downhill since then."

"Please calm yourself," I said. "Relax while I tell you about my younger days in Argentina. Did you know that I grew up in Argentina?"

He shrugged.

"Well, I did," I said. "When I was a young boy, I saw a Purim play about a man who became invisible when someone cast a magic spell on him. There were many people walking in the street, and they all passed him by without a glance. Unaware that he was invisible, the man became very depressed. He sat down on a park bench, despondent, his head in his hands. After a while, the spell wore off, and the man became visible once again. A moment later, someone passed by and greeted him. The man was so delighted with this exceedingly ordinary greeting that he jumped up and shouted a response with an exuberance that still rings in my ears whenever I remind myself of this scene. Even today, fifty years later, I can still hear the joy in that man's heart at being recognized and acknowledged."

The young man gave me a quizzical look. "I don't understand what this has to do with me," he said.

"Oh, it has very much to do with you. You see, it is part of human nature that every person wants to be recognized. The few kind words of an ordinary greeting are very important to people, and what if the greeting were more than ordinary? What if the greeting was warm and loving and full of care and devotion? Such a greeting would be priceless! Do you know why you were so upset when you came home and your wife wasn't there? It was not because of the inconvenience she caused you. It was not because it showed a lack of consideration for you. After all, she is only human. So she was an hour late. So is that such a terrible crime? Are you so perfect yourself? No, my friend, I'll tell you why you were so upset. It was because you felt like that invisible man. You hungered for your wife's warm greeting, and you were deprived of it. Do you understand?"

The young man sat perfectly still, then he nodded slowly.

"You should not take this episode as a reason to be angry at your wife. On the contrary, this hour opened your eyes to how precious your wife's company is to you. You should be dancing with joy for all those thousands of hours that you do enjoy the pleasure and joy of her presence!"

So you see, my son, how important it is to appreciate the blessings of "joy and friendship" and that special "wisdom of caring" that are at the heart of a successful marriage. Otherwise, these wonderful feelings will go as unnoticed as the pleasure of an ordinary greeting is so often overlooked.

Rashi in Bereishis writes that the Creator coaxed Adam to enter the Garden of Eden. Do you understand this? Does a person have to be coaxed to enter a Garden of Eden, a paradise? Why did Adam have to be coaxed? It was because the true pleasures of the Garden of Eden were spiritual. A person is instinctively drawn to material enjoyments, but to seek out spiritual enjoyment takes an intellectual and emotional effort. The Creator told Adam that his concept of divinity would be expanded in the Garden of Eden, and this drew him into the spiritual paradise.

Marriage is both a material and a spiritual Garden of Eden. Therefore, it is important that you appreciate the great spiritual rewards of marriage, the great value of a wife, a family and the *mikdash me'at*, the minor temple that is the Jewish home. When you understand these well, you will gain a full appreciation of the ideal of marriage, and you will be inspired to create it in your own life.

How can you do this? In the following letters, I will give you the benefit of a loving father's advice and share with you some of the teachings and interpretations I have heard from others or learned on my own. The best piece of advice I can give you, however, is to seek out and follow the advice of our Sages at every step of the way. If you do so sincerely, your home will be a true Garden of Eden.

— *1* —

Entering into Marriage

My dear son,

It pleases me very much that you have asked me for guidance in starting off your marriage on the right foot. Many of today's young people think they have all the answers and that their elders have nothing meaningful to contribute to them, but you have shown wisdom beyond your years in seeking advice. My son, I do not have all the answers either, but I can share with you the valuable lessons that my *rebbeim* and my life experience have taught me. I can help you avoid unnecessary pitfalls and pain, and I can help you discover a few truths that will bring love, joy and peace into the beautiful home in which you will raise my beautiful grandchildren.

It seems to me that we should begin with a discussion about love, because the first thing that comes to people's minds when they think about marriage is love. When two people join together for life, when two people merge their lives into one, they surely have to love each other. And who can argue with that? It is definitely true. But what does love really mean? How do we define this love that everyone needs and wants?

Before I begin, let me tell you a story that happened with a friend of mine, a *rebbe* of young boys. This *rebbe* was having a problem with his class when it came to saying *Aleinu* at the end of their prayers. By then, the boys were so fidgety and eager to get to the breakfast table that they just rushed through the words at lightning speed. He would remind them again and again to take their time, but it just didn't do him any good. By the time the boys came to *Aleinu*, it was whoosh and out the door.

One day, the *rebbe* brought a toy cellular phone into the classroom. He sat down at his desk in full view of the boys, dialed a number, waited a moment or two and began to talk.

"Yes, I would like to make an order . . . That's right . . . Please send four pizza pies up to Room 307 in the *yeshivah* across the street . . . That will be cash . . . Is it all right if I pay the delivery man? . . . That's good . . . Of course . . . How long? . . . Just make sure the pizza is still hot when it gets here . . . Thank you very much. Good-bye."

The boys' eyes, bright with eager anticipation, were glued to the cellular phone in the *rebbe's* hand. Suddenly, the *rebbe* opened the toy phone and a little Jack-in-the-box popped out. The class erupted in laughter.

"Did you order a slice for that little fellow, too?" one boy asked as tears of laughter ran down his face.

The *rebbe* smiled and raised his hands for silence.

"All right, all right, everyone. Calm down. We need a little quiet here. Can anyone tell me what was so funny about what just happened? Why was the whole class laughing?"

"It was a joke, *rebbe*," one boy called out.

"Why was it a joke?"

"Because you can't order pizza on a toy telephone!"

"Exactly," said the *rebbe*. "Do you remember learning about the battle against Amalek at Refidim in the desert? Yehoshua and Chur held up Moshe's arms in prayer, and the Jewish people won the battle. Yehoshua saw their prayers answered, and he understood that the Almighty listens to us whenever we pray. But when he came to Eretz Yisrael, Yehoshua saw a very strange sight. He saw people praying to stone idols, and he burst out laughing, just as you boys laughed when I ordered pizza on the toy telephone. Ridiculous! He couldn't believe what he was seeing. And the *Rokeach* writes that Yehoshua was inspired right then and there to write the *Aleinu* prayer, which speaks about how the idol worshipers bow down to 'foolishness and emptiness,' while we bow down to the King of Kings, the Holy Blessed One. How wonderful!"

My friend tells me that *Aleinu* became much more popular in his class after that day. As for the question you would definitely ask me if you were sitting here with me, the answer is yes. After he had made his point, my friend ordered pizza for the class on a real telephone.

So what am I trying to tell you with this story? It shows us that before we can really absorb the great truths of the Torah, we must first expose the 'foolishness and emptiness' of the alternative. Before you can appreciate the wisdom, beauty and durability of the Torah's concept of love, before you can understand the wonderful insights of the Sages into love and marriage, you have to recognize the emptiness and futility of the concept of love that prevails on the street. Oh, their descriptions of love are so full of flowery words, but it is all an illusion, nothing but empty words. So, like Yehoshua, and like my friend in his classroom, I would like to begin by showing you what love is not, and then we will talk about what love is.

Every week, when I come to South Fallsburg, I take a taxi to the *yeshivah*. Usually, I have the same taxi driver, and we converse. He is very curious about all things Jewish, and he always has a bundle of questions for me. One week, he wanted to know my opinion about a more general issue. In a large survey conducted on the campus of a major university, the people were asked to give the meaning of love. Most of the people said, "Love means denying yourself." The taxi driver wanted to know what I thought about this, but I didn't have anything to say. I was puzzled. Why in the world would people think that love means denying yourself?

The Chazon Ish, when describing the various kinds of love, speaks about the love which can emanate from a person's inner strength, leading him to experience kindliness and even feelings of love toward another person at first sight. This love is only the beginning and, as time goes on, it continues to grow. The attraction between a man and a woman is certainly a factor that can help trigger this kind of love. I have also heard in the name of the Chazon Ish that these feelings of instant love may be Divine messages steering people to their intended mates.

However, this kind of love, based on physical desire, has no substance to it. It is not real, and it can evaporate very quickly. A famous writer once wrote that he would stand at the entrance to a subway station and watch the crowds of people coming out. He would catch sight of an interesting woman among the crowds, and he would experience a feeling of affection for her. She would then leave along with all the other people. Ten minutes later, new crowds of people would emerge and, once again, he would spot an interesting woman who would awaken a feeling of affection in his heart. Then she too would be gone. And this could go on and on. New crowds, new women, new feelings. This kind of love comes and goes easily. It is not genuine love.

People in the secular world idealize this type of love, which provides a brief and superficial exhilaration but has no lasting value. They are captivated by the thrill of love at first sight and seek to build relationships that will preserve these emotions over the long term. They consider this the very essence of marriage and, therefore, they are doomed to failure. These emotions evaporate so quickly, and then what is left? An empty shell.

Is it any wonder then that people define love as "denying yourself"? They go into a marriage expecting to enjoy many years of the thrill of first sight, but it doesn't happen. That is not reality. In the real world, those feeling are gone in the blink of an eye, and if they are not replaced by more substantial feelings, the marriage becomes a trap. Husband and wife are very often locked together without any real feeling for each other. How can people endure such a state of affairs? Only by denying themselves, by accepting a situation in which they are emotionally deprived. Love, in their minds, leads to "denying yourself." It is very sad. The first impulses of the heart do not necessarily lead to happiness.

Do you remember our little talk when we prepared your wedding invitation for the printer? I pointed out to you one of the traditional lines, and we talked about it. The classic custom is to describe the *kallah* as the *bas gilo* of the *chassan*, his destined mate. Some people have replaced these words with *bechiras libo*, the choice of his heart. If you recall, I explained to you at the time that "the choice of the heart" is not a particularly solid foundation for a marriage. That first surge of feeling evaporates, and then where are you? The "destined mate" is a much more solid foundation for a marriage, because it brings together two people who are soulmates, two people who will complement each other perfectly in the task of building a warm and loving Jewish home.

In the secular world, marriages built on "the choice of the heart" break down all the time. They are like rotting teeth that need drastic measures such as root canals and crowns in order to endure. Otherwise, the frictions and tensions just keep getting worse and worse. Husband and wife become convinced that they are incompatible, and each conflict that arises adds to their conviction. This incompatibility, when it reaches intolerable levels, often leads to divorce. So, you see, this how people have become conditioned to think. If there is tension, if there is a conflict, it means they are incompatible. This attitude is in the culture, in the very air we breathe, and it is hard to escape it.

Let me tell you a little story.

A woman once called me to discuss her marriage problems. "Rabbi, my husband is impossible," she said. "I have come to the conclusion that we are incompatible."

"Really?" I said. "And what makes you think so?"

All of a sudden, this woman, who was no major Einstein, poured out an amazing stream of technical psychological terms you would have expected to hear from some college professor. I had to hold myself back from asking her what she had been reading and if she could even spell all those fancy words but I controlled myself.

After she hung up, I called her husband to discuss their marital problems. In the course of our conversation, it became apparent to me that there was a financial conflict between husband and wife, and I felt sure that this financial conflict was at the root of their marital problems.

The next day, I called a certain financial planner whom I know to be a clever man. I outlined the financial conflict and asked him to propose a solution. He was silent for a minute or two, and then he suggested a solution that was brilliant in its simplicity and fairness.

That evening the woman called me back to continue our conversation. "Rabbi, last time we spoke," she said, "I got the distinct impression that I hadn't convinced you that my husband and I are incompatible. I gave it a lot of thought, and I think it is important that I give you an in-depth profile of my husband's personality, his neuroses and his compulsive behavior."

"I am eager to hear it," I said, "but could I address a minor issue first?"

"Certainly."

"While I was speaking to your husband last night, I learned, in passing, that you were having an issue with certain financial matters. It happens to be that I am familiar with such situations, and I would just like to tell you what I have heard."

I went on to give her my friend's advice. She listened attentively.

"So that's all I wanted to tell you," I concluded. "All right, now that we have gotten this out of the way, please tell me about your husband's compulsive behavior."

Silence.

"Hello," I said into the telephone. "Is anyone there?"

"I'm here," said the woman in a small voice. "Umm, Rabbi . . . er . . . well, I think . . . You know, as we're talking, I'm thinking about this analysis of my husband, and you know, it . . . I mean . . . I'm not so sure it fits him? I mean he is really such a nice person, you know."

"Then you don't think you are incompatible?" I asked.

"No, I think we are just *perfect* together. We've been talking about building an addition to our house, and he was so nice about it. He is willing to do it just the way it would satisfy me the most. I tell you, Rabbi, I don't know what came over me to say such foolish things to you. Me and my husband incompatible? What a ridiculous idea! Thank you so much, Rabbi, for helping me see everything clearly."

These two people had a solid Jewish marriage based on solid Jewish values. There was no reason that a little conflict should make them think they were incompatible. But the influence of the secular culture is so strong that, as soon as they experienced a little tension, they thought their marriage was falling apart. In the secular world there would have been real incompatibility, because the love that formed its foundation would have long since evaporated. However, this was a Jewish marriage, a Jewish home united with the Divine Presence, with husband and wife bound together with the deepest care and love for each other. There was no incompatibility here. Thank Heaven, I was able to point out a simple solution to their conflict. Then everything fell back into place.

Do not be fooled, my son. The influence of the secular world is very powerful. You have to be on guard against it, at all times.

Let me tell another of my little stories. A rabbi in Denver, Colorado, struck up a relationship with a Jewish man who was really quite far removed from Torah and Judaism. After they became closer friends, the rabbi suggested that this man put up *mezuzos* in his house. The man agreed.

The rabbi ordered the *mezuzos* and had them shipped directly to the man's home. The next day, the rabbi came to help the man put up the *mezuzos*.

Just as he lifted the *mezuzah* and prepared to hammer in the first nail, the rabbi sensed something was wrong. The *mezuzah* felt too light. He opened the beautiful case to look inside. Empty! Quickly, he opened one after the other. All were equally empty.

"What's going on?" he asked the man. "Why are they all empty? Is this how they came?"

"Basically," said the man.

"Weren't there any pieces of parchment inside?" asked the rabbi.

"Oh, those," said the man. "Actually there were little instruction papers in Hebrew, but I took them out. You don't need instructions, Rabbi. You've been doing this stuff for a long time, haven't you?"

A funny story, isn't it? I laughed when I heard it but, afterward, the more I thought about it the more puzzling it seemed. Why would a man make such a mistake? He knows that the *mezuzah* is a religious article. The parchment is written in Hebrew, a language he doesn't understand. Why does he assume so readily that the parchment is an instruction sheet? Why doesn't he consider that it may be a written prayer or that it may have some other religious significance? Why dispose of the papers without even showing them to the rabbi?

The answer is that, according to the secular way of thinking to which he was accustomed, the main expression of value is the external, the superficial appearance. Oh, he understands that religion is also based on higher words and ideas, but the external is primary. When he sees a beautiful case and a piece of parchment, it does not occur to him that the parchment is the religious article and the case a mere receptacle. Instead, he immediately assumes that the beautiful case is the religious article. And the parchment? Why, that must be instructions.

This is how the secular world tries to distort our perception of marriage. They treat it like that uninformed man treated the *mezuzah*. They only see the external, superficial aspect of marriage. The deep inner feelings of caring for a spouse, of giving to a spouse, of loving through giving, these are like insignificant scraps of paper to be discarded. You have to avoid this influence, my son. Before you can absorb the wisdom of our Sages regarding love and marriage, you have to recognize the emptiness of the secular concept of marriage. You have to insulate yourself from the secular ideals and illusions. Only then will you be able to discover the Jewish way.

Remember, my son, marriage is one of the great *mitzvos* of the Torah, and you must study it and work at it, as you would with any other *mitzvah*. No effort is too great, no price too high.

Here is another parallel between a *mezuzah* and marriage. Someone once showed the Brisker Rav a *mezuzah* written in a particularly beautiful script and asked him if it was worth the high asking price. The Rav replied, "No price is too high for a mitzvah performed in the best possible way. It is priceless!" In the same way, my son, no price is too high for the real essence of a marriage, which our Sages expressed in two words — *ohavah kegufo*, he must love her as he loves himself.

∽

My dear son,

When you returned from yeshivah in Eretz Yisrael a few years ago, I was reminded of my own return from Eretz Yisrael some forty years earlier. I remember that summer I spent in Eretz Yisrael with great fondness. Those few months were a turning point of my life.

My memories of the journey home to Argentina are still vivid in my mind. In those days, it wasn't so easy to jump on a plane and fly anywhere in the world, and it was also very expensive. So I traveled by ship, and not a cruise ship with a kosher caterer. Believe me, it was a difficult journey. For nearly a month, I subsisted on bread and sardines. I forgot the experience of a hot meal. I knew that my mother's cooking awaited me at journey's end. I knew she would have all my favorite dishes prepared for me when I came home, and I thought about them a lot when I was chewing my bread and sardines. I could just imagine the savory odors and the wonderful tastes on my tongue.

Then I came home. My parents greeted me with such joy and happiness. My mother made a welcome home party in my honor and, as I had expected, all my favorite dishes were arrayed in front of me. Nevertheless, the feeling of love I felt for my mother was so powerful that all the fine foods were nothing more than background music. Their only value to me at that moment was as another expression of my mother's love for me. I completely forgot about my month-long deprivation on ship.

When you came back from yeshivah — on a non-stop jet flight, of course — I saw the same happiness and excitement in your eyes. The comforts of home awaited you, but it was your eagerness for the loving embrace of your parents that lit that spark in your eyes.

I was reminded of the story with the Berditichever Rebbe. One Friday night after *Kiddush*, he was seated at the table, deeply immersed in his holy thoughts. The *shamash* placed a dish in front of the Rebbe and said, "Fish."

The Rebbe did not respond.

"Doesn't the Rebbe love fish?" asked the *shamash*.

The Rebbe looked up at the *shamash*. "Do I love fish?" he said. "What a question. I love Shabbos!"

That is how I felt about those dishes my mother had prepared for me. Do I love the hot food? What a question. I love my mother!

As much as a child loves his parents, writes the *Rashba* (Responsa 60), the love a man feels for his spouse is much greater. This love does not have to come into being through circumstances and events. It is instantaneous. When a child is born, his parents love him immediately. There is no need to wait until a relationship develops. They love him because he is their child. In the same way, as soon as a man and woman marry, the Creator immediately engraves in their hearts a pure love for each other unequalled in the material world. It is a love so pure and profound that it fills the heart with joy and satisfaction. Under the *chupah* we say, "*Samayach tesamach rayim ahuvim*. Rejoice, beloved friends." When this penetrates to the heart of the *chassan* and *kallah*, when they realize that they are the true "beloved friends," they experience the true immensity of the love the Creator has implanted in their hearts, and the comforts and luxuries of the material world recede in importance. They are no more than background music for the great love that envelops them.

I can just hear the question forming on your lips. You are wondering why "I love fish" is not a pure love but "I love my wife" is a pure love. What is the difference?

Good question.

Our Sages tell us, "If you wish to attach yourself to the love of your friend, occupy yourself with providing benefit for him." Listen carefully to the precise and beautiful wording of the Sages. If you want to "attach yourself to the love of your friend," not if you want to "love your friend."

You can love your friend for many reasons. You can love him because you enjoy his personality. You can love him because you enjoy talking to him. You can love him because he sings beautifully. You can love him for any number of reasons, and none of them will "attach you to him in love." Any love that is dependent on some particular factor is impermanent. If the factors that led you to love him change or disappear, the love will change or disappear.

Therefore, our Sages advised that if you wish to attach yourself to your friend with love, if you want the love to be permanent and indestructible, then be good to him, because such is human nature. We love those to whom we give.

You know, many years ago, when I first started traveling to the mountains every week, the hippie culture was at its height. They used to have their get-togethers in the Catskills, and it was not unusual for me to run across them. I remember getting on the bus one day and noticing a young hippie boy with long straggly hair sitting with a group of his friends. I glanced at them with distaste and found a seat at the far end of the bus.

A short while later, I heard someone clear his throat next to me. I looked up from my Gemara and saw the young hippie boy standing there.

"Excuse me," he said, "do you know what time *shekiah* is? You know, sunset. I have to do Minchah, and I don't want to miss the time."

I looked at him in amazement. "There is still plenty of time until *shekiah*," I said carefully.

He gave me a sheepish look. "Do you mind if I sit down?"

"No. By all means, have a seat."

We spoke for an hour. He told me that he was trying to do *teshuvah*, but he was finding it very hard. I gave him some practical advice, for which he thanked me profusely. He told me he was going to spend Shabbos in a *frum* bungalow colony with which I was familiar, but that he didn't have a *yarmulke*. I took my *yarmulke* from under my hat and gave it to him. He thanked me and went back to his friends. By the way, some time later, I heard from the people with whom he had spent that Shabbos that he was well on the way to a complete *teshuvah*.

After I got off the bus, I found myself wondering about my warm and positive feelings for this boy. When I had first caught sight of him as I got on the bus, I had reacted with distaste. So how was it possible that all of a sudden, I loved him?

Now if I were the Berditichever Rebbe, you could say that as soon as I found out he was Jewish my boundless *ahavas Yisrael*, my love for all Jews, embraced him. Unfortunately, I am not on that level and yet, I felt a genuine love for this boy. What had triggered this transformation?

Then the answer came to me. By being kind to him, by giving him advice, encouragement and my *yarmulke*, I had awakened a love for him in my heart. You love the one to whom you give. That is a real love. When you give to a person, you love that person. When you take from him, you love yourself.

Rav Elya Lapian used to say that a person who says he love fish is really saying that he loves himself. Does he really love the fish? Does he care about the fish? He loves himself and cares about his own enjoyment.

A husband should not love his wife for what she can do for him. That is not called loving his wife; it is loving himself. He should love his wife for herself, because he cares for her. The more he gives to her, the more he will care about her, the more he will love her. And the love that will grow between them is more powerful and joyous than anything else on earth.

Let me tell you a story I heard long ago. On one of my visits to Argentina, I told this story to a group of people just embarking on the road to discovering Judaism, and they were captivated. Of course, I told it to them with many, many details, which I cannot do here, but you will get the idea. It is a truly amazing story.

Dr. Gonzalez was a man in his late forties, a successful physician, a man of the world. He grew up Catholic, the only child of immigrants from Spain who had settled in Argentina after the Second World War.

One time, on a visit to the United States, he passed through the Williamsburg section of Brooklyn on a Shabbos afternoon. It was a scorching summer day, yet he saw many Chassidic Jews walking, wearing heavy fur hats in the sweltering heat.

"So what do you think, my friends?" I said to my audience. "How did our Dr. Gonzalez relate to these Chassidic Jews? Did he identify with them?"

"*Que chiste!*" they said. "What a joke!"

"You are quite right," I said. "Dr. Gonzalez thought the Chassidic Jews were primitive and ridiculous. He could not understand how people could live like this just a few short miles from modern Manhattan. They were like aliens to him — and then an amazing thing happened."

I paused for effect. All eyes were riveted on me. I had caught their attention.

"You see, while Dr. Gonzalez was growing up and pursuing his career, two people in Israel were pursuing a different quest. These were a husband and wife who had lost their child during the Holocaust. When they faced deportation, they had entrusted their little boy to a Catholic family for safekeeping. Miraculously, they had survived the death camps but when they came back for their child, he was gone.

The Chassidic couple immigrated to Eretz Yisrael and settled in Yerushalayim. For the next forty years, they moved heaven and earth to find their son. They wrote thousands of letters and followed up every little clue and lead — until finally, they were successful. They discovered that their son was now a doctor in Argentina by the name of Gonzalez. They made contact with him, sending all the papers to prove that he was only the adopted child of his Catholic parents and that he was actually a Jewish child.

"At first Dr. Gonzalez was skeptical, but the evidence was so conclusive that he was eventually convinced. He flew to Israel to meet his real parents after being separated from them for practically all of his life. The first visit was very emotional, as you can well imagine. It was a time simply to get acquainted. After the second visit, Dr. Gonzalez expressed interest in embracing Judaism and studying the Torah and, wonder of wonders, he was even considering taking on the Chassidic lifestyle!

"Can you imagine such a thing?" I asked my audience. "Here is a man who has been a Catholic since he can remember. He is a modern, sophisticated man of the world, who looked down his nose at the Chassidic people of Williamsburg when he had passed through there, and now, in a matter of days, he is seriously considering the Chassidic life for himself. Does such a thing make sense to you? How can such a thing happen?"

The audience was baffled. No one could even venture a guess.

"I'll tell you how," I said. "It was the love of his parents. When he met his parents and felt the powerful embrace of their love, which had continued burning brightly despite their separation of nearly half a century, he was so inspired and overwhelmed that his whole outlook changed. The Chassidic life may have seemed ridiculous to him before but, if that was the life his parents chose to live, he was forced to look at it from an entirely different perspective to the point that he even considered it as a viable lifestyle for himself."

Can you imagine, my son, how great and powerful is the love between parent and child? Strong enough to change an entire life after two brief visits. Consider then, as I told you before in the name of the *Rashba*, that the love between husband and wife is much more powerful. Think of what a great gift this is for you and your wife. Think of how powerful a force you two have in your possession. If you cherish and nurture it, this love can transform your life and fill it with pure happiness. It can burn with a flame so bright that all the waters of the ocean cannot extinguish it.

Let me ask you a question. The Mishnah in *Avos* (5:1) states that the world was created with ten utterances, each of which represents one of the integrated plans of Creation. One of these plans created the entire animal kingdom. Did you know that there are twenty thousand species of bees in the world? Twenty thousand! And that is just bees. Can you imagine how many species there must be in the entire animal kingdom? The variety and diversity of life is virtually endless, and yet, one plan was sufficient to create it all. At the same time, a separate plan was needed to create the love between husband and wife. Why is this so?

The *Ramchal* explains that a lesser degree of wisdom was required to create the animal kingdom because it has only a temporary purpose and function in life; it has no enduring eternal significance. The wisdom that created man, however, is endlessly profound, because man was created for an eternal purpose. Therefore, to implant the love between husband and wife was one of the great accomplishments of creation. Adam *HaRishon* called his wife "bone of my bones." The *Rashba* understands this as a reference to the instinctive and natural "seeking to benefit the spouse." This is the pure love that God implanted in husband and wife just as surely as He caused their hearts to beat and lungs to breathe. It is the source of the boundless joy that marriage can deliver.

Sometimes, the hardships of life tend to obscure this wonderful love between husband and wife. Stress and problems can aggravate the home situation until this love is all but forgotten. However, no matter how grim the situation the love is still there, and it often takes only a small spark to bring it back to blazing life. In fact, I can recall one couple whose marriage was completely reinvigorated by a simple flu. Tensions in the home had caused the husband to make unreasonable demands on his wife, and eventually their natural feelings of love for each other were numbed. Then the wife came down with the flu. The husband, who was a kind and good-hearted person, took care of her, serving her hand and foot. He could not have been nicer and kinder, and the wife could not stop talking about how wonderful he was being to her. The acts of caring and kindness the husband was performing for his wife reawakened in his heart all the powerful feelings of love he had felt before, and he realized how unreasonable and difficult he had been. A simple flu was all it took.

Sometimes, it takes just a simple act to revitalize the feelings of love so powerfully that the very person is transformed. Let me tell you just this final story before I close this letter.

The Cohens lived in Borough Park. They were quite happy with each other, but when he began to have trouble at work, the home situation also deteriorated. When Mr. Cohen lost his job, things really became bleak at home. He became depressed — and who could blame him? — but that made matters even worse. It was a spiral headed downward.

Then suddenly, in one day, everything changed. The Cohens were invited to a friend's wedding in Philadelphia. Mr. Cohen was too depressed to attend, but Mrs. Cohen refused to stay at home. She got a ride with a friend and left for the wedding. A little while after she left, Mr. Cohen noticed that she had prepared her favorite wedding dress but had forgotten to take it. He thought about how distressed she would be when she got to Philadelphia and realized she had forgotten her dress. He jumped into his car and hurried off to Philadelphia, arriving there just as his wife was stepping out of her friend's car. He ran to her and placed the dress in her hands.

You can imagine the scene that followed. She was so overcome with his thoughtfulness that she couldn't stop thanking and praising him. The love in their eyes shone so strongly that a teenage girl standing nearby asked her mother if this husband and wife were newlyweds. Right there on that sidewalk in Philadelphia, their love blazed up in full force and enveloped both of them with sheer happiness and joy.

Mr. Cohen felt so marvelous that he snapped out of his depression and, with a fresh positive outlook, he found an even better job within a short time. The home situation returned to wonderful. He had hurried to Philadelphia to help his wife, but he himself had been the greatest beneficiary of his kindness.

Think about all this, my son, when you feel the warm presence of your wife in your home. Your love for your wife and your wife's love for you are your greatest treasures.

My dear son,

Did I ever tell you about my next door neighbor in Argentina? He was a boy my age, and we went to public school together. I had a lot of trouble with him, because he was completely non-observant. There was no indulgence that he denied himself, and he used to tell me all the time that by adhering to the Torah, I was missing out on the best things in life. He would speak about his exploits and adventures as if they were the greatest achievements to which a person could aspire in life.

Well, life has its little ironic twists and, one day, I heard him singing a completely different tune. You see, his sister married a boy who had been raised in an observant home although he himself was no longer observant. Out of respect for his parents, who were quite simple *shomer Shabbos* people, the wedding and the week of *sheva berachos* were conducted strictly according to tradition. My neighbor returned from the Shabbos *sheva berachos* so inspired that he could not stop talking about his sister's parents-in-law.

"The way these people look at each other after so many years of married life," he enthused. "It's incredible, like they're living in a paradise."

Believe me, this kind of long-lasting love between husband and wife is a rarity in the outside world. People who witness it are amazed. My parents used to take frequent walks in a park near their home. They would stroll together and chat, enjoying the beautiful outdoors and each other's company. One day, a park attendant stopped them and said, "I've been watching the two of you for a long time. Tell me your secret. How is it possible to be so happy together after so many years?" It is a real puzzlement to people who are drawn together by superficial feelings and are forced to live with disappointment once those feelings evaporate.

This is not our way. The Torah tells us (*Bereishis* 24:67) that "Yitzchak brought [Rivkah] to the tent of his mother Sarah, and he took Rivkah, and she became his wife, and he loved her." Look at the sequence of events. He took her to be his wife and he loved her, not the other way around. Rav Shamshon Raphael Hirsch points out that this is the formula for Jewish marriage. The marriage plants the seed of love, and the shared experience of giving to each other, of building a family together, of fulfilling the *mitzvos* together, of growing together in appreciation of the goodness of the Creator, these produce a deep-rooted love that flourishes and blossoms and bears the most wonderful fruit. Every shared event —

every birth, every family celebration, every marriage of a child, every Shabbos when husband and wife sit together at the table like king and queen — all of these add more blossoms of love to the flourishing tree of the marriage. This is why the love in a Jewish marriage keeps growing and deepening with each passing year.

I want to quote to you from a letter by Rav Akiva Eiger, the great genius of Torah, the heroic leader of his generation who was able to cope with adversity and crisis. He wrote these words some time after his wife passed away. "After she departed from this world, in my profound pain and sorrow, I was left without joy. I felt weak and infirm. I was unable to eat or drink. I could not keep my food down, not even for a minute. I could barely find the strength to say the *berachah acharonah*. Sleep eluded me, even though I took medications. Thank Heaven I have recovered a little, but I still feel too weak to concentrate properly on my prayers or to learn in depth, even a simple piece of Gemara."

What was the essence of this deep love? Rav Akiva Eiger describes it in a few words: "The A-mighty very kindly blessed us with good children and grandchildren. She walked down with me to the *chupah* of our son and also the *chupah* of our daughter with joy and happiness." With these simple words, he captured the essence of their love. Let me explain.

In our hectic world, the details sometimes obscure the truly important things in life. When a child is engaged to be married, there are a thousand things that must immediately be considered. The date for the wedding. The availability of the hall. The things that must be bought. The arrangements that must be made. The caterer. The flowers. The photographer. Clothing for the family. An apartment for the new couple. And on and on. And of course, the expense. Where will the money come from? All these things crowd in on your thoughts and feelings, and perhaps you forget to express your appreciation properly to the Creator. Perhaps you also miss the opportunity to savor the deepest emotions between husband and wife that emerge at times like these.

This is what came to my mind when I read Rav Akiva Eiger's letter. The love between husband and wife evolves from shared experiences and shared accomplishments. When husband and wife walk a child down to the *chupah*, when they have succeeded in nurturing him through childhood and adolescence, instilling in him a profound love for the Creator and His Torah and *mitzvos*, it is a moment of supreme accomplishment by husband and wife together. This is the highest expression of love in a Jewish marriage. This is real love.

As I thought more deeply into these few, simple but oh so powerful words in Rav Akiva Eiger's letter, it occurred to me that walking a child down to the *chupah* was just an example, the most extreme example, of the expression of love between husband and wife. The truth is that these kinds of moments really happen all the time, on a smaller scale.

How about when husband and wife wish each other a good year on Rosh Hashanah? Isn't this a moment full of reflection on the efforts and accomplishments of the whole year? Isn't this a moment of shared hopes and visions for another year of accomplishment that lies ahead?

How about when husband and wife sit together at the Seder table and listen to their young child say the *Mah Nishtanah*?

How about when husband and wife sit together in the *succah* after working so hard to build and adorn it?

How about the ordinary moments that come up in everyday life that are so full of extraordinary meaning and emotions?

One of my more vivid memories is a winter night when I was working late to prepare a *chaburah* to say in the yeshivah the next day. Your mother didn't finish her work either until very late. As you would expect, we were both exhausted when we retired for the night.

We had just fallen asleep when the baby started to cry. I opened my eyes and saw that your mother was already up and going to the baby. She worked her magic and the baby went back to sleep. But a short while later, he was up again and crying. This time, I jumped out of bed as soon as I heard him and let your mother sleep. After I put him to sleep, I returned to bed. But wouldn't you know it? It wasn't long before he was crying again.

This time, we both got up, nerves on edge, and tried to calm him down together. After a few minutes, he relaxed and gave us the sweetest smile you've ever seen. We looked at each other and realized how blessed we were. Our baby was happy, which made us happy. This special moment of happiness, which was ours alone, produced another blossom on the tree of our love, right then and there at that extraordinary ordinary moment.

Let me leave you now with an interesting thought, a nice metaphor for the love in a Jewish home. You know, when you take a plane trip, the plane starts off slowly on the runway and then it gathers speed. You feel the rush of speed, and then you're airborne and you don't feel it anymore. It almost feels as if you're standing still. But then the captain comes on the public address system and announces the speed, and it's much faster than the plane's speed on the ground when it was taking off. You may not feel it, but you know you're traveling fast.

It is the same in marriage. While you were meeting your *kallah*, getting engaged, getting married and enjoying your time as newly-weds, you felt the quick speed of emotions rapidly accelerating. Don't think, however, in the years that follow as time flies by, that you are at a standstill. On the contrary, you are traveling more quickly than ever. The home you are building together, your shared accomplishments, keep growing faster and stronger day by day, and your love for each other is flourishing and blossoming all the time.

My dear son,

The Midrash (*Vayikra Rabbah* 5:8) tells an interesting story about a fellow who managed the estate of a great nobleman. He was having a difficult time and desperately needed an infusion of new funds to make the estate prosper. Although he was deeply concerned, he put on a good face and buoyed up his spirits. He groomed himself carefully, combed his hair, washed and pressed his clothing and put on his adornments. Then he went to see the master of the estate.

"So how are you doing?" asked the nobleman as soon as his manager came in.

"Excellent!" said the manager.

"How is the land?"

"Bursting with fruit."

"And the livestock?"

"You should eat your fill of their fat."

"And the produce?"

"Plentiful."

"Hmm. Do you need some more capital? How much?"

"Ten gold coins would be just fine."

The nobleman handed the manager the money. "Here they are. Had you asked for twenty, I would also have accommodated you."

So what do you think, my son? Do you think this nobleman was a naïve fellow, easily fooled? Not at all. He was an exceedingly clever man. He understood that a manager who remained in good spirits when going through difficulties was just the kind of man who would run a profitable estate. Even if he encounters difficulties he will not lose himself, and he will find the solutions he needs. He will be successful.

A marriage works the same way. The force that will crown marriage with great success is a positive outlook, the profound belief that marriage is the passageway to a lifetime of joy and happiness and the confidence that the blessings of love and companionship will grow from day to day and year to year. If this is your outlook, you will not be discouraged by the occasional snags you encounter in the lifelong journey of your marriage.

My grandmother lived well into her 90s long before it was common to do so. One day I told her about an acquaintance of hers who had passed away in her 70s.

"Oh," she said, "she was an old lady."

At the time, I thought this was a strange remark for a 90-year-old to make about a 70-year-old. Years later, I learned the answer. The Creator implanted in human nature the desire to live forever. As long as a person's desire to live is strong and vibrant, he is forever young. When that desire wanes, he becomes old. My grandmother was younger at 90 than the other woman at 70.

However, this innate emotional desire to live forever needs the counterbalance of an intellect that understands rationally that the future is finite, and that we will not live forever. Using the analogy of a car, the emotions serve as the gas pedal and the intellect as the steering wheel and the brakes. When the two are combined, the result is a functioning automobile. In people as well, the combination of the emotion and the intellect results in a complete, fully functioning person.

The same can be said about a marriage. The emotions are the engine that drives the marriage, giving it the vigor, vitality and sense of excitement that keeps it fresh and exhilarating. However, without the intellect, it will run out of control and perhaps crash, Heaven forbid. The intellect adds a dose of realism and pragmatism to a marriage. It searches the horizon for obstacles and pitfalls, and it draws on the wisdom of our Sages to find the best way to steer around them. The proper balance between these two elements the emotions and the intellect, will result in a happy and harmonious marriage.

You need to be aware, my dear son, that life is not always one happy experience after another. You open a family album and turn the pages, and all you see are smiling faces. Those are the moments we want to capture forever, but there are other moments as well. You rarely see pictures of pain and grief and loneliness, but these are an equal part of life and, by extension, of marriage. You and your wife need to learn to share all the experiences of your lives, the ups and the downs, the joys and the sorrows, in a way that will deepen the bond of love and companionship between you.

— 2 —

Made in Heaven

My dear son,

I told you about my friend the *rebbe* in one of my earlier letters. He has a gift for getting through to problem children. He was telling me the other day about a boy named Moshe, whose parents are divorced. The boy is a handful in school, which is not unusual for a child who has grown up watching his parents fighting with each other all the time.

One day, the *rebbe* was teaching the class about Eliezer and Rivkah, and he told them that Eliezer came to Aram Naharayim by *kefitzas haderech*, supernatural transportation.

All of a sudden, young Moshe raises his hand. "*Rebbe*, I have a question," he said. "What is the speed limit of *kefitzas haderech*?"

Trouble.

But my friend is an expert at handling trouble. "Good question, Moshe," he said. "You know, boys, the trip to Aram Naharayim and back by camel caravan should really should have taken months. But it didn't. Soon after Eliezer left, Yitzchak stood in the fields and prayed with all his might that the Creator should help Eliezer find his preordained mate. And the Creator answered his prayers. As soon as Yitzchak finished his prayers, he looked up, and there were the camels bearing Rivkah and Eliezer approaching in the distance. But wait! How did they get there so fast? Had Eliezer simply gone around the block and found a girl to impersonate Rivkah? So Eliezer told him that he had enjoyed *kefitzas haderech*, and this was indeed Rivkah. At that moment, Yitzchak saw with perfect clarity that his match was made in Heaven."

"What about my question?" said Moshe.

"I'm getting to it, Moshe," said the rebbe. "When Eliezer came to Aram Naharayim, the first girl he saw was Rivkah. What if he had come a few minutes later? He would have missed her! Then he would have been left standing at the well asking all the other girls to water his camels, and nothing would have happened! So you see, Moshe, it was important that he arrive at that exact second. This means that his *kefitzas haderech* had to operate at a specific controlled speed to make sure he came exactly on time."

An amusing story, but it also contains an important lesson. It shows us how a *shidduch* works. The Creator coordinates and synchronizes everything so that the *shidduch* successfully comes together.

How do we know this is so? It was proven by a famous experiment.

The Midrash tells us (*Vayikra Rabbah* 8:1) about this experiment. A Roman noblewoman asked R' Yosi bar Chalafta, "Now that He has finished creating the world, what does the Creator do all the time?"

"He makes matches," he replied.

"That's all?" she said. "I can do the same. I have so many slaves, male and female. I can pair them all off, in one hour."

"Well, perhaps it is an easy thing for you to do," said R' Yosi, "but the Holy Blessed One considers it as difficult as the splitting of the sea."

So he left her and went away. What did she do? She summoned a thousand male slaves and a thousand female slaves and ordered them to line up in parallel rows. Then she said, "This one should marry this one, and this one should marry this one." In one night, she had them all paired off.

They came back to her the next morning, this one with a bruised skull, this one with a damaged eye, this one with a broken arm and so on.

Immediately, she sent a message asking R' Yosi bar Chalafta to come.

"Rabbi, it is true!" she said. "Your Torah is beautiful and praiseworthy. Everything you told me was right."

This is the famous Midrash. R' Yosi tried to convince the Roman noblewoman that matching up couples was as contrary to nature as splitting the sea, but she refused to believe it. Only when her efforts resulted in total chaos and mayhem did she admit that R' Yosi was right.

Think, my son. Why do our Sages report this experiment? Obviously, they consider it proof of the truth of the Torah. But is it really proof? Was the experiment conducted properly? After all, what did this Roman noblewoman do? She took a thousand male slaves and a thousand female slaves and matched them up, slapdash, in one night. A thousand matches in one night! One night! She could have put a little more effort into her matchmaking. She could have tried to match up people who were compatible. So did the failure of her thousand random coupling prove that a more methodical person could not be a successful matchmaker?

This woman apparently thought that peace and harmony between spouses is the natural condition. She knew, of course, that marriages sometimes don't work out, but she assumed that those were the exceptions to the rule. All thing being equal, she believed, it was so natural for a man and a woman to be together that all problems would work themselves out. If so, all she had to do was match her slaves randomly, and she could safely assume that most of them would be happy.

To her shock, however, she discovered that none of them was happy. R' Yosi had been right! Putting together a man and a woman was against nature, like the splitting of the sea. So how are there any successful marriages, at all? It must be that the Creator pairs them together. It is obviously true that, as the Torah says, "*mei'Hashem yatzah hadavar*, the matter was ordained by G-d." As the Gemara states (*Sotah* 2a), "Forty days before the child is formed a Heavenly Voice declares, 'The daughter of this one is for that one.'" This is the beauty of a Jewish marriage. It is part of the Creator's master plan. He designed a certain man and a certain woman to be husband and wife despite the unnatural nature of random marriage, and He brought them together to live in harmony, peace and joy. This is what the Roman noblewoman proved with her experiment.

You may wonder why the Midrash needed to bring this story to prove its point that marriages are made in Heaven. Why wasn't it sufficient to bring the *passuk* I just mentioned or one of the numerous other *pesukim* in the Torah that indicate the Divine origin of marriages? The Midrash is writing to faithful Jews to whom a *passuk* is a proof. Why do we need the story of the Roman noblewoman?

It was simply to give graphic form to the concept in our minds, to help us feel that which we already know. You know without a doubt that there is a place called Alaska, but it is quite different when you travel there and see it with your own eyes. When you hear about those thousand couples who were at each other's throats after just twelve hours of marriage, you can understand how fortunate you are that the Creator Himself has included you in His master plan and found for you a spouse whom He designed especially for you. There will surely be many times that you will fail to see or understand the workings of this master plan in your life, but the assurance that it exists will forever be engraved on your heart.

My dear son,

Let's talk a little more about the Gemara's statement that matches are preordained from the womb. You know, if you were to ask people when a *shidduch* is born, some might say that it is when the idea of the match takes root in the mind of the matchmaker. But this, of course, is not so. It is born well before the *chassan* and *kallah* are born. The Tashbatz explains that, at the moment of conception, the Almighty instills in the man and in the woman a predisposition to come together in harmony and build a dwelling place for the Divine Presence. This preordained couple is born with personality factors that make them perfectly matched to each other. Now, you may not see any extraordinary factors in these two people that make them so perfectly complementary, but believe me, they are there.

When I was growing up in Buenos Aires, there was a terrible tragedy. Within a short time, a family lost two children because of the Rh blood factor. Do you know what that is? There is a certain factor in the blood called Rh. If both parents are Rh positive or Rh negative, the children will be fine. But if one parent is positive and the other negative, the children are in extremely grave danger. Well, these two children died, and I remember attending their funerals. It was terribly sad.

These days, you don't hear about too many such cases. People are more aware of the problem, and they take preventive measures. Now, I don't think you'll find many non-medical people who will be able to explain the nature of the Rh factor, but everyone knows that such a thing exists.

It is the same with the personal factors in the marriage. Even though you don't see them, they are there. When the Roman noblewoman threw together two people, their factors were not aligned and the matches were not successful, to say the least. But when the Holy Blessed One brings two people together, you can rest assured that their factors are in alignment, and that they are a perfect match.

The Tashbatz makes another important point. Although a person's match is preordained, he explains, we are all free to marry whom we choose. Marriage is a *mitzvah*, and as with all *mitzvos*, we have free will as to how, when and with whom to perform this *mitzvah*. No one will force us to do anything against our will, not even the Creator. Nonetheless, the Creator brings together these two people, the only two people perfectly matched with each other, to build a private dwelling place for the Divine Presence, and He puts them into situations where they will find each other. Of all the millions of people in the world, He arranges that these two people should meet each other. Is it incredibly amazing? It is as amazing as the splitting of the sea.

For myself, I feel a great sense of encouragement from the knowledge that the Creator watches over us so carefully. It gives me a sense of security, not only about my marriage but also in all aspects of my life.

The Chafetz Chaim taught us to use new technology to bolster our faith in our Father in Heaven. Recently, when a friend gave me a ride in his car, I had the opportunity to take the Chafetz Chaim's advice. My friend had a new device in his car called a GPS (Global Positioning System). This is a computer connected to satellites that track the position of his car at all times and let him know where he is. If he needs directions to get somewhere, the computer will give him directions and guide him to his destination. Every street he passes, every exit on the highway, is identified on his screen. I had never seen such a device, and it made a deep impression on me. I was reminded of the Mishnah (Avos 2:1) that warns us, "Be aware of what is above you. An eye that sees and an ear that hears!" Here was a graphic example of "an eye above that sees." What a perfect way to remind ourselves that the Almighty sits above us and watches us with "an eye that sees," that He guides and steers every step of our lives.

What was this device called? I supposed it would be called "Seeing Eye" or "Eye in the Sky," but no. It was called "Never Lost." I shook my head in wonder. Why was it called such a name? Could it be used only by people who are lost? Surely, it had much wider use than that.

Then I thought about it some more, and decided that "Never Lost" was a good name after all. Even if a person is not lost, the most important benefit of this spectacular little device is the knowledge that it will help him find his way regardless of where he wanders; that no matter where he finds himself, he is never lost. The way back may be complicated and lengthy, but the "Never Lost" computer will lead him back to safety and security.

I want you to know, my son, that you have a "Never Lost" computer to guide you in your marriage. It is the teachings of our Sages that provide you with the wisdom of the Torah at every step of the way. Your emotions may take a wrong turn, now and then. You may occasionally wander off the straight and true path of your relationship with your wife. Nevertheless, the teachings of the Sages, if you seek them out, will always bring you back. You will never be completely lost. It may take a long time. It may take hard work. It may call for a lot of patience. It may require that you reach into yourself for hidden reservoirs of understanding, care and concern, but the route will be clearly marked. Follow the teachings of the Sages, and you will never go wrong. They are the road map to the success of your marriage. They are your "Never Lost" computer, programmed by the Creator Himself.

This is the key, my son. You must have trust and faith in the Creator. Always remember that He has made you and your wife for each other, and He has guided both of you through life so that you will meet and find each other. If you always remember this, your marriage will be successful. You will know that the problems that arise can be worked out, and you will seek guidance in the "Never Lost" computer the Creator has provided for you — the teachings of our Sages.

Trust and faith, my son, trust and faith. When I was a teenager in Argentina, a member of our small congregation, a man who fulfilled the Torah and *mitzvos* on a very minimal level, lost a child to leukemia. I remember going to his house to offer my condolences. The people in the room sat for a while in silence. What could you say? Then it was time for Minchah. To this day,

I cannot forget how this man said the Kaddish for his child. His voice was breaking with emotion, yet bursting with unquestioning faith in our Father in Heaven. I saw how his suffering and loss had elevated him and brought him closer to the Creator, and I was deeply moved.

A woman recently called me to complain about her marital situation. It did not take more than a minute or two for her to burst into tears. I could not imagine what deep, dark secrets she was about to reveal to me. But when she got her emotions under control and began to tell me her story, I was utterly amazed. This woman had everything in her marriage that one could want. What's more, the Divine master plan that had brought her and her husband together was a marvelous story. And yet she was crying bitterly. Why? Because her wonderful husband was not the prince of her fantasy.

I spoke about the undeniable Divine providence that had led to her marriage. I spoke about her husband's goodness and sterling qualities. I explained to her how clear it was, despite any notions she may have gotten into her head, that she and her husband were created especially for each other, that they were perfectly matched and that their life could be a paradise if she would only allow it to happen. It was useless. She was lacking in her faith and could not appreciate the opportunity for blissful happiness that was within her grasp.

I did not know this woman, and we never spoke again. When she hung up, I felt a heavy sadness. And I wondered why some religious, faithful people find it so hard, even when the evidence is staring them in the face, to accept the idea that marriages are made in Heaven, as our Sages have taught us.

I don't really have a good answer, but an interesting thought occurred to me. Very often, you will hear someone get up at *sheva berachos* and make a speech in honor of the *chassan* and *kallah* in which he proves by *gematria* that the numerical values of their respective names are equal and that they are therefore clearly meant for each other. Of course, the numerical values are hardly ever equal, so he will engage in some mathematical gymnastics by throwing various other elements into the mix, such as last names, places, *pessukim* and phrases. If this doesn't do the trick entirely, he can rely on *gematria* devices such as the *mispar katan* and the *kollel*. And when he finishes with his convoluted calculations, he announces proudly that they were obviously meant for each other.

These speeches are very nice entertainment. They are bright and colorful, matching the festive paper goods on the table. However, they also contain an element of good-natured mockery, and I think that exposure to this type of mockery diminishes our ability to accept preordination with complete faith.

The idea that husband and wife are made for each other, that the match was preordained from the womb, is not just an interesting tidbit of information, a subject for light conversation and banter. It is the foundation and bedrock of a successful marriage, the key to enjoying a lifetime of marital bliss and to building a Jewish home that is a paradise in every sense of the word.

Open your heart to this important concept, my son, this critical element in our Jewish faith, that marriages are made in Heaven, and you will enrich your life and fill it with happiness and joy.

My dear son,

Many people don't realize that the Creator's idea of a marriage made in Heaven may not be the same idea as theirs. They construct fantasy spouses in their minds and decide that these are the spouses that are perfect for them. They decide that this is their marriage made in Heaven. Otherwise, they turn away.

A young man once told me that he had been invited to the home of a certain family for a dinner. This was a prominent and wealthy family, and they had a daughter of marriageable age. The young man was convinced that they had an interest in him as a prospective son-in-law, and that the daughter in particular was interested in him. I happened to be quite familiar with these people, and I knew they would never consider this young fellow a suitable match. But he was thoroughly convinced that this girl was his preordained bride.

I asked him to sit down with me and learn a certain Gemara in *Mo'ed Katan* (18b). Rava once overheard a man praying for a certain woman to become his wife. "Don't do that," Rava told him. "If she is preordained for you, you will not lose her. And if she is not, then you will come to deny the Creator." Rashi explains that when his prayers go unanswered he will think the Creator does not hear him.

"I don't understand something," the young man said to me. "We don't tell people not to pray for a *refuah sheleimah* when they are sick. We are not concerned that they will deny the Creator if their prayers might not be answered. Why is praying for a certain wife different?"

"So what do you think?" I asked him.

"Perhaps because it is such a simple thing," he said, "that we feel sure He will do it. And if He doesn't, we get upset."

"You may be right."

"That is how I feel about marrying into this family," he said, "but I suppose one never knows what will be."

"Exactly," I said. "Sometimes the marriage connection is obvious, but sometimes, it is much more complex. The Gemara gives a number of sources for the concept that marriages are made in Heaven. One is the marriage of Yitzchak and Rivkah, which is a pretty clear connection. The Gemara also brings the marriage of Shimshon, the great judge of Israel, and a Philistine woman named Delilah, and here the connection is not so clear any more. In fact, it is quite perplexing. However, the Creator has His grand schemes, and we cannot expect to fathom His plan. Just because you think a match is perfect for you, my young friend, is no proof that it is."

The Dubno Maggid has an interesting explanation for the "fantasy *shidduch* made in Heaven." When you see an arrow protruding from the bull's-eye of a target, does it mean that an expert archer shot it? Not necessarily. If the target had been there before and the archer had directed his arrow right to the center, that would be proof of his expertise. But an archer can also shoot an arrow into a plain piece of wood and then draw concentric rings around the arrow to give the impression that it was shot into the center. Then it is no proof of marksmanship. The same is true with a *shidduch*. A person can conjure up an image from his fantasy and then draw concentric circles around it and proclaim it is preordained. It means nothing.

There can be many causes for these fantasy images. It may be a meeting with a girl who makes a positive impression but declines to continue. Or it may be images engendered by the mass media. These images befuddle the mind and make people forget simple common sense.

An old man has a problem with cataracts in his eyes. He is told that the lenses of his eyes will be replaced by artificial lenses and that his vision will be cloudy at first. He will have to go through a period of adjustment until his vision returns to normal.

The old man seeks out a hospital that has the best state-of-the-art equipment and the finest doctor in the field, and he has his cataracts removed. When he awakens from his operation, his vision is cloudy, and he gets upset. "What kind of a doctor is he?" he fumes. "He made a mistake on my eyes. He put in the wrong lenses."

Where is this man's common sense? He knows that the doctor is the finest in the field. He knows that his equipment is the best in existence. He knows that it is perfectly normal to have cloudy vision after the removal of cataracts, but when he experiences discomfort, all logic goes out the window and he is ready to accuse his doctor of incompetence.

The same is true with some married couples. They get married, and things are a little rocky. Immediately they are convinced they made a mistake, and that they married the wrong person. Don't they realize that they may need a period of adjustment? Don't they realize that it can take a little time for two people to adapt to each other? They experience discomfort and impatience, and their common sense goes out the window.

The problem is that they have built up in their minds fantasy images that crowd out their common sense. The Sforno writes that the Serpent that led Chavah to sin, the evil inclination, is the *dimion*, the imagination. The evil inclination creates mirages for us, images with no connection to reality, that lead us deep into the barren wastelands and leave us there to rot. The evil inclination tries to make us react like a thirsty wanderer in the desert who sees the green oasis shimmering on the horizon and rushes towards it, only to find nothing but hot sand. So too does the evil inclination try to fill our minds with images that do not exist, so that we will be lured to pursue them and disregard the wonderful matches that the Creator has prepared specifically for us.

It is important to recognize this, my son, and to hold on to your common sense at all costs. The Creator made you and your wife for each other and brought you together because you are perfect for each other. If you understand and appreciate this, you will surely find all the happiness that is in store for you in your marriage made in Heaven.

— *3* —

A Rose in Full Bloom

My dear son,

Not too long ago I was giving a talk in the yeshivah about Aharon's methods for resolving disputes. Our Sages tells us that he used to go to one of the combatants and tell him, "My son, your friend is so troubled by this fight you are having. His heart is full of remorse. He is really ashamed of what he has done, and he would never do it again. He really cares about you, and if you would take a good look at him, you would see what a fine fellow he is. He wants nothing more than to make up with you and become good friends." He would continue talking to this fellow until he "removed the jealousy" from his heart. Then he would go the other fellow and give him the exact same speech. And it worked! The next time these two people would meet they would embrace with warmth and love.

A young fellow in the yeshivah came to me the next day.

"I don't understand something," he said. "I have two roommates who fight like cats and dogs all day, every day. Believe me, they're just totally impossible. So after I heard yesterday about Aharon, I decided to try the same thing. I went to each one and told him that the other one was sorry for everything he ever did and said, and that he wanted to make up and be friends, but it didn't help one bit. They just laughed in my face. I don't understand it. Why didn't it work?"

I smiled at him. "Tell me," I said, "when you told your roommate that the other fellow repents and is ashamed for what he has done, did you really believe it yourself?"

"Of course not," he said. "The other guy blames him for all his problems."

"There you go," I said. "If you don't believe it, how do you expect your friend to believe it?"

"So how did Aharon do it?" he asked.

"If you notice," I replied, "our Sages speak about Aharon talking to one of the combatants until he removed the jealousy from his heart, not the hatred. Hatred is a superficial expression of the emotions. It can come and go in the blink of an eye. But jealousy is a deeply rooted emotion. A person who is jealous of another distorts his image until he sees only the negative and none of the positive. Then he feels justified in hating him. Aharon, however, had such love for his fellow Jews that he saw straight through to their goodness. He was able to help each combatant get beyond the distortions and see a clear image of the other. He helped them recognize the goodness in each other and realize that there was no basis for jealousy and hatred. This was a rare skill, my young friend. I'm not saying you can't acquire it. You can. However, it is not as simple as going from one to another and telling them something you yourself don't believe."

According to our Sages, Aharon applied his skills and techniques to marital problems as well. He was the first Jewish marriage counselor! The daily stresses of life can lead to misunderstandings and friction between spouses, and there descends between them a fog that obscures their wonderful qualities from each other. This, of course, leads to even more friction, and the situation deteriorates. Aharon, with his ability to see the true goodness in everyone, would help husband and wife penetrate this emotional fog and see clearly once again each other's true feelings and fine qualities. He helped them move on and make a new start.

Our Sages further tell us that Aharon never told either of the spouses, "You have done something wrong. You are at fault." At first glance, this seems strange. How could he reconcile their differences without pointing out the fault where it lay?

But after thinking it over, it made perfect sense to me. I reminded myself of the time I had flown on a plane at night. As I looked out the window, all I could see was inky blackness. And then, as the plane began to descend, I saw lights. Thousands of lights. Millions. Suddenly, there was a gleaming, brilliant landscape below me when before there had been only darkness.

Now imagine that I was sitting next to the pilot in the cockpit, and I saw that he is steering the aircraft to the left, away from the dazzling lights of the city toward the blackness beyond. Do I need to say to him, "Sir, I believe you are making a mistake"? or would it be enough to say, "Sir, look at all those beautiful lights to the right"? The message will come through loud and clear, and he will undoubtedly correct the flight path and turn the plane in the right direction.

This is how Aharon treated a husband and wife who were experiencing marital difficulties. He worked to reawaken the deep love spouses feel for each other and bring them closer together, by pointing out their wonderful qualities and their profound devotion to each other, despite all the difficulties they were having. Gently and kindly, by pointing them toward the light and away from the darkness, he coaxed them back onto course without ever telling them outright that they had wronged their spouse.

You know, it is interesting that only with regard to marital disputes do our Sages tell us that Aharon never said, "You have done something wrong." It seems that when he came to make peace between friends, neighbors or business associates, he would indeed tell the one or the other, or sometimes both, that he had done something wrong. He put on his extra-sensitive kid gloves only when he was dealing with disputes between husband and wife.

I think this is because the attachment between husband and wife is so close. The *Tosafos* (*Kesubos* 4a) tells us that husband and wife are so closely bound to each other that this itself can sometimes lead to misunderstandings and friction. The feelings between husband and wife are so deep and so intense that they know intuitively what the other feels. There is no need to tell a spouse something like, "You did something wrong," just as there is no need to tell it to the pilot. All you have to do is to talk about the strong bond of love between them, and everything will be corrected without having to spell it out.

Two friends or associates, however, know perfectly well that they are two completely different worlds, no matter how close their friendship or association. Therefore, even if they are very angry with each other, it is still possible to say to the one or the other in the most gentle of terms, "I think you made a mistake here. It seems that the problem is basically your fault, and you really should take the initiative in rectifying it."

My son, do not be upset if I speak to you about these things. I know perfectly well that your marriage is a happy one. I can see it in the shine in your eyes and your wife's eyes. It warms my heart and makes me very happy. But these things I am telling you are important for every married person to know. We don't fill our tanks after we've run out of gasoline. In the same way, it is important to work on seeing one's spouse in a positive light when things are going well. After all, my son, it is always wiser to avoid your problems than to solve them.

My dear son,

A *rosh yeshivah*, traveling to a wedding, was seated next to a gentile on a plane. The gentile asked him where he was going. The *rosh yeshivah* told him, and they chatted for a few minutes about weddings in general.

As they were parting, the gentile said, "By the way, enjoy your wedding."

The next day the *rosh yeshivah* spoke to his students about the difference between the Jewish and gentile attitudes toward weddings. "To a gentile," he said, "the wedding is a party, just another occasion for a celebration and having a good time. To a Jew, a wedding is a holy moment. Certainly, we feel joy and we celebrate but, for us, the wedding is an opportunity to provide an additional dwelling place for the Divine Presence in a new Jewish home. For us, it is the joy of a sanctified moment rather than a good time."

"I don't understand," one of his students said. "How does our dancing at a wedding bring the Divine Presence into the new Jewish home?"

"I will explain it to you," said the *rosh yeshivah*. "It is because the Divine Presence only rests in a state of joy. We find that the prophet Elisha called for a musician to play for him so that he would be in a state of mind that could accept prophecy. There are three partners in the Jewish home. The man, the woman and the Divine Presence. When we sing and dance for the *chassan* and *kallah*, we add to their joy and thereby make their home a worthy dwelling place for the Divine Presence."

A beautiful thought, don't you think?

So we launch this new Jewish home with a rush of joy. We help make it a suitable dwelling place for the Divine Presence. And then what happens? Times get hard. Relationships become strained. And what happens to the joy? What happens to the Divine Presence?

The joy is always there. The great fountain of joy that allowed the Divine Presence to come into the Jewish home never runs dry.

Shlomo HaMelech writes (*Shir HaShirim* 2:1), "I am like the young rose of the Sharon (*kachavatzeles haSharon*), like the rose of the valley (*shoshanas ha'amakim*)." Shlomo HaMelech is comparing the Jewish people to a young rose and to a rose of the valley. What is the difference between the two?

The rose is a wonderful flower. When I was growing up in Buenos Aires, I used to spend a lot of time in a park that was full of roses. I can still remember the delicious fragrance. The beauty and fragrance of those roses would fill me with an inner harmony. However, not all the roses were so beautiful and so fragrant. The younger roses were wrapped in green leaves, obscuring their beauty and depriving them of the dewy moisture that brought out their sweet scent. Nonetheless, I knew the potential of those young roses. I knew that when those green leaves would fall away, the rose would blossom and achieve its full beauty and fragrance.

The Jewish people, declares Shlomo HaMelech, are like roses, fragrant in their holiness and good deeds. Sometimes, however, they are like young roses, oppressed by their surroundings and difficult times, wrapped in the green leaves of adversity, and their beauty and fragrance are diminished but they are never lost. When the Creator relieves the severity of our plight, we blossom and flourish, and the Jewish soul bursts forth with songs of praise to Him. We become like the rose of the valley in full bloom, aglow with the special beauty and fragrance of the Jewish people.

It is the same in a Jewish marriage. The bond between husband and wife is like the most beautiful rose and, when it is in full blossom, it becomes a thing of beauty, fragrance and transcendent joy, a fitting dwelling place for the Divine Presence. But the fate of marriages, like the fate of the Jewish people, can take a turn for the worse. Whatever the causes — friction, financial pressure, problems with family or children — suffocating green leaves can wrap themselves around the marriage, and suddenly the beauty, fragrance and joy are no longer in evidence. Nonetheless, they are still there. There is still a beautiful rose under those layers of oppression. Those green leaves can be peeled away, and the rose can be brought back to full bloom. That is a gift from the Creator, the promise of everlasting joy in a marriage. The relationship may seem stale and lifeless, but a little effort can revive it. The bond of love is so strong and the fountain of joy so deep, because this relationship was made in Heaven by the Creator Himself.

There was a doctor who used to live near us. You won't remember him, because he moved to California before you were born. We were quite friendly, and we often talked about the wondrous ways in which the Creator had formed the human body. A patient of his once had a liver operation, and this led us to speak about the incredible ability of the liver to regenerate. You can remove part of a liver, and it will grow back to its original size. All wounds heal by a process of regeneration, by which the body makes repair tissue, but the liver in particular has the ability to regenerate itself, even if part of the organ is missing. It is really amazing.

Well, he moved away to California, as I mentioned already, and I didn't see him again for many years. One day, he appeared on my doorstep with a very serious look on his face. He had come to talk to me about his rebellious son, who had run away from home. He needed advice.

"Do you know where he is?" I asked.

He nodded.

"Have you spoken to him?"

He nodded again.

"And?"

He shrugged. "He just refuses to come home. What am I supposed to do? Drag him? Call the police?"

"Let's talk."

We spoke for about two hours about his home life and his son, and it became abundantly clear that my doctor friend and his wife had not been getting along for twenty-five years. They quarreled incessantly, and it was not at all surprising that their son had decided to flee from the battlefield.

"My dear friend," I said. "The best and possibly the only way to bring your son back home is to restore peace and harmony to your home."

He sat bolt upright. "You don't know what you are saying. We're talking about twenty-five years of fighting. Twenty-five years! Do you expect us to turn things around so that everything is sweetness and light? You can't be serious."

"But I am serious. If you want your son back, you have to fix your marriage. There are no two ways about it. You cannot expect him to jump back into the caldron from which he has fled."

"But, rabbi, the chance of love in our marriage is dead. You hear me? Dead! Dead! We've learned to live together after a fashion. We've worked out a system of sorts. But love? Serenity? Harmony? Be serious, rabbi."

I closed my eyes and thought for a moment. How could I convince him that there was still hope for him and his wife? And then I remembered. "Do you recall a conversation we had many years ago about the liver?"

"The liver?" He looked at me in a strange way. "What about the liver?"

"You explained to me that the liver is a regenerative organ. Even if part of it is missing, it will regenerate and grow back to its original size. The Jewish marriage is also a regenerative organ. No matter how badly it is damaged, it can be brought back to life. That is how the Creator made it. He blessed it with deep, inexhaustible wellsprings of love and joy. If you dig down far enough, you will find them, and your marriage will become once again like a rose in full bloom, fragrant and beautiful to behold. Remember how you used to give your liver patients hope and encouragement? Well, now is the time to accept some of that hope and encouragement for yourself. Go home. Sit down with your wife and talk about it. You will see. She will be glad to renew your marriage and rekindle the flame of your love. And then your son will be eager to come home."

He gave me a long look, and then he nodded. We shook hands, and he left. A few weeks later, I heard that their son was home again.

⚬

My dear son,

I want to add a small thought to my previous letter. You know, sometimes these letters become so lengthy they become like chapters in a book, so I thought I had better stop. I also thought it might be nice to end on such a positive note, you know, about the boy coming home after his parents repaired their shredded marriage.

In that same context, I also wanted to mention an interesting *Kli Yakar* in *Parashas Yisro*. The Torah tells us that Yisro "heard" and came. What did he hear that moved him to come? Our Sages tell us that he heard about the splitting of the sea. What is the connection? The commentators offer many solutions. The *Kli Yakar* offers an original insight.

When Moshe first went down to Egypt, he brought with him his wife Tzipporah and his two young sons, but Aharon suggested that he send them back to Midian. What was the point of bringing more Jews to Egypt when they were trying to remove those that were already there? So Moshe sent her back with the children. According to some opinions, he divorced her. So back in Midian, Yisro was sitting with a divorced daughter in his house. When he heard that the Jewish people were coming out of Egypt, the thought crossed his mind that maybe he should try to get Moshe and Tzipporah back together again, but his emotions and feelings led him to dismiss the thought. Reconciliation after divorce was impossible, he thought. After all, could a broken relationship be revived in a marriage of the same beauty as the original? Such a thing could surely not be.

But then Yisro heard about the splitting of the sea. The entire sea had split down the middle, both sides completely separated from each other. And then the two sides had come together, bringing the sea back to the state of its original normalcy. This incredible phenomenon inspired him to rethink his perspective on marriage and consider the possibility that the marriage could be restored to its original beauty. And so, he decided to bring Moshe and his daughter back together again.

We Jewish people are not dependent on the instinctive emotional reactions of the outside world. We are the people who experienced the splitting of the sea, and we know perfectly well that a marriage can always be restored to its original beauty. Sometimes, it may be quite easy to do it and, sometimes, it may take an enormous amount of work. But goodwill on both sides, perseverance and a lot of prayer can restore any Jewish marriage so that it is once again like a rose in full bloom.

My dear son,

When you see two elderly people who are obviously happily married for many, many years in peace and harmony, would you think that theirs is a perfect marriage? Would you think that nothing could be done to improve it?

If you said "yes," I'll prove to you that you're wrong. When the angels came to Avraham to bring the good tidings that he would have a son, they asked him, "Where is your wife Sarah?" Rashi explains that they knew perfectly well that Sarah, in her modesty, had stayed in her tent, but they wanted to show Avraham that they were aware of Sarah's exemplary modesty. Why did they want to do this? Rashi says that it was "*kedei lechavevah al baalah,* to make her more beloved to her husband."

Avraham and Sarah were in their nineties. They were well aware of each other's sterling virtues, and they held each other in the highest esteem. Yet, the angels felt it was important to point out their appreciation of Sarah's modesty and thereby awaken a new stream of love in Avraham's heart. Do you see how delicate the marital emotions are?

You cannot put a marriage on cruise control once you've brought it up to a good level and expect everything to hum along nicely without any additional effort. It just does not work like that. The feelings of the marriage have to be renewed and refreshed constantly.

Every Friday night, we say, "*Lecha dodi likras kallah*. Let us go, my beloved, to greet the bride." We welcome every Shabbos as a *kallah*, a bride, not a wife. R' Tzaddok explains that every Shabbos must be viewed as a renewal of holiness, and it must be greeted with renewed feelings in our hearts.

It is the same with marriage. You must always look at your wife as a bride, and you must keep your feelings for her fresh and vigorous. For the rest of your life, you must continue doing and saying things that will revitalize your love — even when you will both be in your nineties!

The Gemara explains (*Niddah* 31b) that the monthly separation between husband and wife is to reinforce their love for each other, so that the husband will feel as strongly for his wife as when "she walked down to the *chupah*." This is clearly not referring to physical attraction, but to the emotional and spiritual bond between husband and wife. The initial attraction flares quickly and is extinguished as quickly. In reality, Achashverosh should have quickly gotten tired of Esther, but the Almighty miraculously caused his love for her to endure. The Gemara states (*Yoma* 29a) that Achashverosh loved her as "during the first hour." Do you see the difference in the expressions? "The first hour" is clearly a physical attraction, and it took a miracle to preserve it. "When she first walked down to the *chupah*" is pure holiness.

The Yom Kippur *machzor* describes the glow on the *Kohen Gadol's* face when he came out of the Holy of Holies at the completion of the service. So what metaphor does the *machzor* choose to describe this glow? It was like a "*chassan* emerging from his chupah"! The *machzor* cannot find an image with which we are familiar that is closer to the holy glow on the *Kohen Gadol's* face, than the glowing face of a *chassan* emerging from his *chupah*.

I remember R' Aharon Kotler's face on Yom Kippur, aflame with purity and holiness, and I understand how difficult it is to describe it to someone who has never seen it. But the *machzor* chose an image everyone knows, the glowing face of a *chassan* on the pinnacle of holiness, standing beside the soul mate the Creator of the Universe has prepared especially for him, building the sanctified temple of his own home, his heart filled with happiness, joy and the most profound gratitude to the Creator. His mind, heart and soul are suffused with prayer as he extends his humble welcome to the Divine Presence to enter his home and to bestow upon it happiness, peace and the blessings of children, life and livelihood.

Think about it. You are familiar with the glow of holiness and pure joy on a *chassan's* face. This is the image that the *machzor* compares to the *Kohen Gadol* on Yom Kippur.

This is why the Torah wants the monthly separation, to preserve the feeling "of a *chassan* greeting the *kallah* under the *chupah*." We see that when the Almighty created Chavah for Adam He could have presented her to him just like that. He would turn around, and there she would be, his smiling wife — but that is not what the Almighty did. According to the Midrash, He adorned Chavah with twenty-four ornaments and brought her to Adam under the *chupah*. A simple presentation would not have delivered everlasting happiness. Only the special aura of *chassan* and *kallah* standing together under the *chupah*, their hearts and souls bound together forever, could bring them together in everlasting happiness.

This is the feeling you must try to capture and preserve and constantly renew in your marriage, especially after the monthly separation. You are forever *chassan* and *kallah*, the two of you together, meant for each other, standing side by side under the *chupah*, separated from the rest of the world.

I see that this letter is also beginning to run overtime, so I'll just conclude with a story about the Klausenberger Rebbe. After the liberation of the concentration camps, the Klausenberger Rebbe opened a yeshivah for young survivors.

One time, the Rebbe met a boy who had abandoned the path of Jewish tradition during the Holocaust. He observed nothing. The Rebbe invited the boy to join his yeshivah. The boy protested that he had no intention of doing any *mitzvos*, but the Rebbe reassured him that it was all right. He could come anyway. So the boy came, and true to his word, he did not put on *tefillin* or do any other *mitzvah*. Nonetheless, the Rebbe showered him with fatherly love.

One Friday afternoon, the Rebbe sat down with the boy and spoke to him about his mother lighting Shabbos candles. The Rebbe spoke with such warmth and emotion that the boy's heart melted, and he broke down into uncontrollable tears. The Rebbe hugged him and let him cry himself out. From that day on, the boy turned his life around. He went back to full observance and became one of the best students of the yeshivah.

Notice, my son, that the Rebbe never rebuked him and never said a harsh word to him. He won him over with pure, sincere love. It takes a special wisdom to understand that nothing is more effective than love.

Whatever differences there may ever arise between you and your wife, remember this story of the Klausenberger Rebbe. The best way to resolve them is by treating each other with pure love, sincere love, unlimited love, the love of a *chassan* for his *kallah* when he is standing under the *chupah*, the love that makes a marriage like a rose in full bloom.

— 4 —

Hidden Feelings

My dear son,

Have you ever read Rabbi Michoel Ber Weissmandl's classic book *Min Hameitzar*? It is his memoir of his experiences in Nazi-occupied Slovakia during the Holocaust, an extraordinary book, full of *emunah* and *yiras shamayim*. If you haven't read it yet, make it your business to get hold of a copy. It would be worthwhile to make the effort.

In this book, Rabbi Weissmandl writes about his efforts to save his Jewish brothers and sisters in nearby Poland from the Nazi killing machine. On one particularly dangerous mission, he was captured by the Nazis and taken to the office of an infamous Nazi butcher named Fokola.

"Who are your associates, Weissmandl?" Fokola demanded.

Rabbi Weissmandl remained silent.

"Tell me their names or I will kill you right now," said the Nazi killer.

Rabbi Weissmandl still remained silent.

"If you don't answer me right now," hissed Fokola, "I will have you and your entire family sent off to one of those camps in Poland you're so worried about, the ones from which no one ever returns. And I'll do it today, before the sun sets. Speak to me! Who are your associates?"

Rabbi Weissmandl was desperate. He was ready to sacrifice his own life, but the lives of his wife and children? What was he to do?

He looked up at his brutish Nazi tormentor and began to speak about the suffering of the Jewish people in Poland. As he spoke, an emotional dam within his heart burst and his words poured forth in an impassioned voice about the misery and torment of the Jews of Poland. The tears flowed from his eyes as he described the pain and suffering under the inhuman treatment of their tormenters. How could he sit back, he asked, and do nothing while his innocent people were dying and suffering all around him?

When he finished, he looked up and was shocked to see that Fokola's eyes were also moist with tears.

"All right, Weissmandl," he said gruffly. "You can go. But don't let me catch you again!"

Rabbi Weissmandl was shocked that this cruel anti-Semite, this heartless murderer, had actually shed tears over the plight of the Jews of Poland. This episode taught Rabbi Weissmandl the awesome power of human tears. When he had broken down and cried, his tears had touched the Nazi and unearthed some spark of mercy buried deep in his heart.

Why are tears so powerful? I think it is because tears are the most eloquent expression of profound pain and suffering. As much as you try to describe what you are feeling inside, you cannot bring across to another person how deeply you are hurt, but when you cry, when you shed tears, your hurt is visible for others to see. The harder you cry, the more tears you shed, the deeper the hurt. When your pain is so visible, even a brute like Fokola cannot help but be affected if there is still the slightest trace of humanity left in his heart.

Babies and young children cry often, and sometimes quite hard, even when their suffering is not so great. Since they have no other way of expressing what they feel, they use their tears to alert their parent to their physical and emotional needs. As they grow older and learn to cope with their little pains and discomforts, the frequency of their tears diminishes.

But what about frequent tears in an adult? What does that mean? Some people are inclined not to take frequent tears seriously. They view them as a childish reaction, as a response to the many small pains and discomforts of daily life, just as babies cry often when they are hungry or otherwise uncomfortable. In reality, however, this is rarely the case. Frequent tears in an adult are a sign of a deep and abiding hurt that flares up again and again. When an adult cries, there is almost always a terrible hurt behind it.

The Ponovezher Rav used to describe his first encounter with the Chafetz Chaim. When the Rebbetzin opened the door for him, he heard terrible crying and screaming, as if a great calamity had happened. He turned to the Rebbetzin with a look of consternation on his face.

"Don't be afraid," she reassured him. "That is my husband you hear. He is praying for a woman who is having a difficult childbirth."

I do not know if the Chafetz Chaim was an overly emotional person. I would not think that he cried easily. But I do know that he felt every Jew's suffering as deeply as he would his own. I do know that when he suffered, he cried.

You know, my son, and so do I, that women cry more frequently than men. That does not necessarily reflect an emotional immaturity. It is because they are more sensitive and they feel things more deeply.

A few weeks before I was married, I was waiting my turn near the public telephone in the yeshivah. The young man on the telephone was obviously speaking to his wife, and I could hear through the receiver the faint sound of her crying. The young man listened quietly and rolled his eyes in frustration, as if to say, "Oh no! There she goes again."

I have to admit that ∇ considering that I was soon to be married ∇ this little episode made me nervous. What was I getting into? Is this what marriage was all about? I looked around in the *sefarim* and found that the Maharal discusses just this topic.

The Maharal explains that the tendency to cry frequently is common in married women because of the paradox of their situation. On the one hand, a married woman is in a position of prestige and dignity. She is the *akeres habayis*, the mainstay of the home, the queen of her family, beloved and respected by her husband and children, important in her own right. At the same time, she feels dependent on her husband for her emotional support. This dichotomy in her status make her particularly sensitive to every word her husband says to her, and to every gesture and look he casts in her direction. Therefore, if he says an unkind word to her or offends her in any other way, it upsets her equilibrium and causes her untold pain. Her husband's insensitivity can shatter her world. For this reason, concludes the Maharal, our Sages tells us that *"le'olam yehei adam zahir beona'as ishto*, a man should always be especially careful not to cause anguish to his wife."

As a young child I spent the summer in a camp on a farm in Argentina. One of the boys in my group had allergies and would consistently sneeze. There was an old peasant who worked on the farm who was annoyed by this almost incessant sneezing. He insisted that the boy was sneezing to gain attention, and berated him for it. Our counselor took the ignorant old peasant aside and explained to him in great medical detail about allergies and invisible irritants in the atmosphere. The peasant listened wide-eyed. All this information was clearly a revelation to him. From then on, he never bothered the sneezer any more. He understood and sympathized.

When a husband sees his wife crying often, he should not become irritated with her, as the old peasant became irritated with the boy who used to sneeze a lot. Rather, he should try to discover which irritants are causing her to cry and do his best to remove them from the presence of the most precious person in his life. It is surprising how much a little effort and sympathy can accomplish. Most likely, he will be able to help her remove the irritants. And, if he cannot, at least she will have his emotional support.

⌒

My dear son,

The Satmar Rav, R' Yoel Teitlebaum, and the Viener Rav, R' Yonasan Steif, both lived in Williamsburg and were very close. One Friday night, they were discussing a certain issue on which they had a difference of opinion, and the Satmar Rav made a remark that seemed a little too sharp.

Later, after the *seudah*, the Satmar Rav told his *shamash* to get his coat. He was going to Rav Steif's house to apologize. The Satmar Rav put on his coat and, accompanied by his *shamash*, went out in to the street. To his surprise, Rav Steif was waiting for him in the street.

"I knew you would come to apologize," he said to the Satmar Rav. "So I decided to wait for you here. Why should you have to walk all the way to my house?"

An amazing story, isn't it? I cannot promise you that this story actually happened, but I do not think such a story can be made up.

Regardless of whether it is a true story or not, there is a beautiful lesson to be learned here, for every husband and wife. These two *gedolim*, the Satmar Rav and Rav Steif, held each other in the very highest esteem. They were extremely sensitive to each other's honor and prestige. Nonetheless, it can happen that one would inadvertently utter a remark that might offend the other. Such a thing is possible, and when it occurred to the Satmar Rav upon reviewing their conversation in his mind that his statement might have been offensive, then his reaction was to seek out Rav Steif right away and apologize. As for Rav Steif, he understood that an apology would be forthcoming, and he did what he could to make it quick and comfortable. Beautiful!

The same applies to husband and wife. There is always a possibility that you may inadvertently offend your wife. Because of her higher sensitivity, as we discussed in the letter, she will probably feel a deeper hurt; she may even cry. My son, condition yourself to apologize immediately. Do not let her stew in her pain for even one extra instant. Believe me, you will be the beneficiary. By always apologizing right away, you will give her a wonderful sense of security, and she will be thankful to you for it. What's more, I wouldn't be surprised at all if she followed Rav Steif's example and did everything in her power to make it easy for you to apologize. It will become a natural reaction for both of you. As soon as you sense that your wife has been offended, the apology is forthcoming and will be readily accepted. Such a marriage is a true Garden of Eden.

So how do you know when you have offended your wife? This is something you will figure out by being open-minded and attuned to her feelings. One thing is for sure. You cannot use yourself as a measure. If a certain remark would not offend you, do not assume that it would not offend her.

Think back to when you were a rough and tumble little boy romping with your friends. You used to shove each other and scream and yell, and it was all part of having fun. Imagine if you had behaved that way to your sister (and I'm sorry to say that sometimes you did). There is no way your sister would have considered such behavior fun. She would have considered it violence, no less.

A friend of mine who doing his medical internship in a military hospital told me about a soldier who was awaiting surgery for kidney stones. The soldier was doubled over in pain and screaming his head off. My friend tried to soothe him with gentle words, but the soldier continued to scream in his pain. My friend did not know what to do for the stricken soldier.

The door opened and the chief surgeon walked in to check on the patient before the surgery.

"Lie down, soldier," he said with quiet firmness, "and be still."

It did not help. The soldier continued to scream hysterically.

The surgeon slapped him on the shoulder. "Private!" he said. "Lie down right now, and stop this ridiculous screaming. Be a man!"

Instantly, the screams came to a stop. The soldier lay down on the bed, with only a slight grimace on his face to indicate that he was still in pain.

You see what's going on here? My friend couldn't get anywhere with the soldier, because he spoke to him gently and soothingly. The soldier did not relate to that kind of talk, and he continued screaming. The chief surgeon, however, treated him like the soldier he was. He slapped him on the shoulder and told him, "Be a man!" This style and language got through to him, and he was able to bring himself under control.

Now imagine, my son, if this had been a woman suffering from kidney stones and screaming with pain. I don't think the chief surgeon could have stopped her screams by telling her, "Be a man!" Or even, "Be a woman!" However, gentle, soothing words might have been very effective.

The Rambam says (*Mishneh Torah, Hil. Ishus* 15:9) that a man should always speak gently to his wife. This one seemingly simple rule is so important. You cannot talk to your wife as you would talk to your friends. Even among refined men, there can be a certain rough edge, a bantering tone to the conversation. It is natural and inoffensive. To men! But to women, it is poison. If you talk to your wife in that way, she will be hurt and offended, and you may be bewildered by her reaction. Do not be bewildered. Remember this important lesson. Speak to her gently. It is the only way.

My son, I know you so well that I can already hear your response. Tell me if I am right. "So what do you expect me to do?" you are saying. "Are you telling me that I cannot be natural with my wife? Are you telling me to speak in a way that is not really me?"

No, my son, I am not telling you to be anything other than natural. I am telling you to develop two naturals. I was once listening to a tape of a lecture. The speaker began in Yiddish and then switched to English for some reason. Perhaps he was more comfortable in English and just got tired of the Yiddish. Anyway, I noticed an interesting thing. While he was speaking in Yiddish, his tone was humble and refined, but when he switched to English, he became rough and proud.

How do you explain this? It occurred to me that this man really had two sides to his personality. He was naturally proud and rough, but he had developed a more humble and refined side in his contacts with his rabbis and teachers. When he spoke English, his old habits came to the fore, but when he spoke Yiddish, he instinctively identified with his rabbis and teachers, and his more refined side came to the fore.

You can do the same, my son. You can develop a softer, gentler side, and whenever you talk with your wife, that side will come forward. You will speak softly and gently, and you will find that you very rarely make any inadvertent remarks that she might consider offensive.

Try it out, my son. It is really not that hard to do.

My dear son,

Just a few more thoughts about the importance of developing a special language for when you communicate with your wife. We spoke about the need to avoid all the rough and ready type of talk so common in banter among men. We spoke about learning to communicate in softer, gentler tones. There is one more point I want to add.

It has to be natural. As you said in those words I put into your mouth, "Are you telling me that I cannot be natural with my wife?" No, my son. On the contrary, I'm telling you that you cannot be anything but natural with your wife.

Let me tell you an interesting story about the famous *tzaddik* R' Elya Lapian, the *Mashgiach* of Kfar Chassidim. His weekly *shmuessen* were full of fire and *yiras shamayim*, and they had a profound effect on the students of the yeshivah.

Naturally, R' Elya delivered his *shmuessen* in Yiddish, his usual language. Over time, however, many Sephardic boys started coming to the yeshivah, most of whom really had to struggle to decipher the Yiddish. R' Elya realized he was being unfair to the Sephardic boys, and he began to say his *shmuessen* in Hebrew. Strangely enough, the Sephardic boys complained. They wanted him to go back to speaking in Yiddish.

Do you understand such a thing? It seems that it makes no sense, but it really does.

You know, when Yosef's brothers came to Egypt to buy grain, he recognized them but they did not recognize him. The Torah states (*Bereishis* 42:7), "And Yosef saw his brothers and recognized them, and he estranged himself from them (*vayisnaker aleihem*)." *Targum Onkelos* translates *vayisnaker aleihem* as "and he thought out everything he said to them." Yosef knew that if he spoke to them naturally, his personality would come through and they would recognize him. Therefore, he made a special effort to compose and construct every sentence he said to them, and in this way he was able to disguise his identity.

When R' Elya spoke in his natural Yiddish his whole heart and his holy personality flowed into his impassioned words. The Sephardic boys may not have understood every word he said, but the feeling and the message came through, loud and clear. R' Elya moved and inspired them even when they did not understand every word he said. But when he spoke in Hebrew, measuring every word and translating the Yiddish into Hebrew in his mind, the emotions and personality were no longer there, and the effect was lost.

In the same way, my son, it is not enough to translate your mode of masculine speech into the gentler form more appropriate for your wife. If you must constantly translate, your personality and warmth will not come through, and you will not be able to communicate properly. That is not good. No, my son. You must make the effort to learn her language, to become fluent in it, to speak it naturally without "thinking out everything you say to her."

So how do you learn to speak her language naturally? The first step is to understand the components of her language.

Let me tell you the fundamental difference between the way men and women communicate. Men separate the intellectual from the emotional. They consider them two distinctly different issues and are inclined to deal with them separately. They will argue and discuss the logic of a situation without considering its emotional implications in the context of the same discussion. When they have figured out the logic, the intellectual component of the issue, then they may or may not consider the emotional component. Very often, the emotional component is resolved by itself once the intellectual issues are resolved. Women, however, need to deal with the issue in its entirety. They cannot separate the intellectual and emotional components. To them, the two components are inextricably intertwined.

This is where the frictions arise. Men work things out between themselves on the intellectual level. Even when the discussions get heated and angry, the focus remains an intellectual one. Women work things out between themselves by dealing with the issues globally. Husband and wife, who are essentially capable of a much closer relationship than with others of their own gender, have to learn new communication skills. The husband is intent on resolving a problem by analyzing it with cold, logical reasoning. The wife, however, needs to have the emotional angle taken into the equation, and she may find her husband's purely intellectual approach insensitive and even offensive. How do they get together?

One of them has to give way, and the responsibility is on the husband. The wife cannot be expected to disregard her emotions; dealing with the intellectual component alone will never satisfy her. For the husband it is more a matter of style. There is nothing wrong with dealing with the intellectual and emotional components at the same time. Doing so will not leave him dissatisfied. It is simply not his style. Well, he can make it his style. He has to be sensitive and attuned and work at it deliberately until he make it his style, until it becomes a language in which he is really fluent.

Our Sages tell us that "a man has an obligation to make his wife happy." This means that it can be done. The Torah does not impose impossible obligations on people. Every man clearly has the tools to develop new communication skills. Every man can learn how to address his wife's inner feelings and emotional needs and make her genuinely happy.

My dear son,

I want to give you one very sharp example of how a man speaks to men in one way, but absolutely must not speak to his wife in the same way.

When I came to the Lakewood Yeshivah, I overheard a conversation between two non-Jewish workers. One had been working there for years, and the other was new.

"Look at those Jewish boys," the new worker said. "They fight and yell at each other like I never saw. They stand there over their books and they bang their fists on those wooden stands and they stamp their feet — and they yell! Oh boy, do they yell. I tell you, when my friends get into a brawl in the bar, they don't yell like these boys do."

The older worker laughed. "You don't understand nothin'," he said. "These kids ain't fightin' with each other. They's just arguin' about the holy books. You see 'em come out after they's finished and watch 'em go to lunch together, and they's the best of friends."

When young men in the yeshivah argue over a *sugya* or the interpretation of a *Rashi*, there is absolutely no animosity between them, only love. Both of them are seeking the objective truth of the *sugya*. By reinforcing his side of the argument with a few well-placed shouts, each one hopes to bring the other one around to the other point of view or at least stimulate him to make a better argument to defend his own position. When they close their Gemara, they walk together arm in arm out of the *beis midrash* the best of friends, their friendship reinforced by an invigorating, purely intellectual debate.

Now let us imagine that one of these young men goes outside, and his wife is waiting for him in the car. She is a new driver and not very confident about her skills on the road. They chat happily as she drives. Suddenly, a car cuts into the lane in front of her. She swerves around the car without looking to her left. There is a loud screech of brakes as a car she had not noticed makes a short stop to avoid hitting them. She pulls over to the curb and breathes hard as she tries to calm down.

Now let us imagine two scenarios. In the first, the husband tries to explain to her what she did wrong and what she should have done under the circumstances. She finds it hard to admit that she was wrong. She insists that it was the fault of the other cars. For the sake of safety, he feels it is important to convince her that she was in the wrong and that she must avoid such mistakes in the future. Instinctively, he sets about convincing her in the same manner he tried to convince his friend in the yeshivah that his interpretation of the *sugya* was correct. He makes many logical points and argues heatedly until he is sure that it must be crystal clear to her. When she still does not concede the point, he yells for emphasis.

So tell me, my son, do you think this would work? Of course not. But why? All right, let us see what he is actually doing. No matter what crystal clear logical points he is making, she is hearing that he is upset and ashamed of her incompetence. If she felt insecure before, she feels even more insecure now. And she also feels that her husband is not pleased with her. And she feels that her husband cares only about his needs and not about her feelings; that he is selfish. This conversation has not gone well. It has accomplished nothing constructive. She has not absorbed his corrections, and friction has been introduced into a happy marriage. Not good.

Now, let us consider an alternate scenario. The first thing her husband tells her is that she definitely has driving ability, and that it will improve greatly with experience. He then agrees that other drivers on the road are often careless and do other dangerous things. Then he tells her that, for her own safety so that she should not get hurt, Heaven forbid, and for the safety of her passengers, she should learn certain defensive techniques. Then he offers to explain them to her. He can do it now, but if she is too rattled, he can do it later. She feels secure, confidence and self-worth are reinforced, and she gladly accepts his criticism. Much better, wouldn't you say?

Your wife is not your *chavrusa*. You cannot pound away at her as you would at your *chavrusa*. It is wrong. And it is also useless.

My dear son,

I hope you gave a little thought to my last letter. Knowing you, you probably had a good laugh here and there, which is fine. But I am sure you also took it seriously. It really is a very important point, especially for a husband who has spent some serious time in a yeshivah.

One last thought on this topic.

I hope you're not getting tired of my little stories about Argentina. Well, here is another one. You remember that I used to take a yearly trip to Argentina to visit my parents. Now, Argentina is a long way from the New York area, and generally, you have to catch a connecting flight in Rio de Janeiro, Brazil. On one of my return trips my connecting flight was delayed, and I had a little extra time in Rio de Janeiro. I decided to look around in the airport shops for some trinkets to bring home for the children.

As I passed by a jewelry store, the proprietor, noticing my beard and black hat, came out and addressed me in Yiddish. We chatted for a while. Then he spoke to me about his merchandise, and before I knew it, I had bought a bracelet for your mother.

How did he manage to do that? Now, I don't mean that your mother doesn't deserve a nice bracelet. The best is not good enough for her. But at that particular time, the idea of buying a bracelet did not even enter my mind. I was looking for simple trinkets, and yet, I bought a bracelet. How did the proprietor, a complete stranger, convince me to do it?

Let me tell you what occurs to me. At the end of *Bereishis* (50:21), after Yaakov had passed away, Yosef's brothers are concerned that he will take revenge on them. Yosef reassures them. "He pacified them, and spoke on their hearts." Rabbi Shamshon Raphael Hirsch points out that the Torah does not say that he spoke "to their hearts (*el libam*)" but "on their hearts (*al libam*)." What does this mean? It means that Yosef spoke words that exerted an influence over their emotions and thereby pacified them.

Rashi, based on the Midrash, tells us Yosef's exact words. "If ten candles could not extinguish one candle, how could one candle possibly extinguish ten?" In other words, if you brothers, who collectively possess so many merits, could not overwhelm me with my few merits, how could my few merits overwhelm all of your many merits? If the Creator saved me from you, He will certainly save you from me. You don't need to worry.

Listen to Yosef's wisdom. He built up their confidence by telling them that they had so many merits, that they were still men of stature. He spoke "on their hearts"; he exerted an influence on their emotions. Then he told them he would take care of them, and they were reassured.

This is also what the Jewish jeweler in Rio de Janeiro did with me. First he spoke to me in Yiddish, making me feel a bond with him as the only two Jews among so many gentiles; he found a way to exert an influence over my emotions. Then he spoke about his merchandise and noticed a spark of interest when he mentioned the bracelet. Aha! There was the bond between us, and there was the buyer's interest. From there, it was not that difficult for a skilled merchant to close the deal.

When you want her to understand the situation from your perspective the first thing you have to do is let her know that regardless of who is right or wrong on this particular issue, you think she is wonderful, the most important person in your life. Then think deeply into the issue and see if you can find even a slight advantage to her in coming around to your point of view. Once she is reassured that her status in your eyes is secure, and once she is convinced that the solution you suggest will be beneficial to both of you, you will be surprised at how easily the issue will be resolved.

Just one thing. Be honest with yourself. After all, it is possible that she is right and you are wrong. In that case, give in gracefully right away.

— 5 —

Man or Macho

My dear son,

When I was growing up in Argentina fifty years ago, the level of observance was very low. A boy who wanted to live an observant life, with a serious commitment to keeping all the *mitzvos*, would encounter difficulties from his family and friends, but that was just the least of it. When the time came for him to marry, it was almost impossible for him to find a young woman willing to commit to that kind of lifestyle.

I knew a young fellow who was seriously committed to a life of Torah, and not surprisingly, none of the local young women considered him a suitable prospect for marriage. He could not even get a young woman to consent to meeting him. The years passed, and he remained unmarried. However, he was strong and determined in his convictions, and refused to compromise.

One day, as if by a miracle, a wonderful young woman agreed to meet him. He was overjoyed. During their first meeting, he could not contain himself and limit his conversation to light topics. He could not avoid talking about the issues that were important to him. Since she was similarly interested in observance, the conversation progressed quickly. Then he told her that he wanted his wife to cover her hair after they were married. She smiled politely, and the conversation moved on to other issues.

The next morning, the young man received a call from the *shadchan*. The young woman had enjoyed his company, but she absolutely refused to see him again. She would never — absolutely never! — even consider covering her hair.

Undaunted, the young man called her again that evening. In a sweet, gracious but firm manner, he suggested they meet again on the following night. She readily consented. They continued to see each other and were eventually married. She did indeed cover her hair, and together, they happily built a home in which the Shulchan Aruch reigned supreme.

How do you explain such a mysterious development? I remember hearing about it at the time, and how baffled we all were at her behavior. Why did she see him again after having given such a firm refusal to the *shadchan*? Why didn't she just say, "No," and hang up the telephone?

Let me tell you what I think.

The Ramban in *Bereishis*, in discussion regarding Chavah's eating from the Tree of Knowledge, makes an important observation. He writes that a woman naturally "yearns very much for her husband" as a source of leadership and guidance. This is part of the very essence of womanhood. She is all-loving, all-embracing, the gracious queen of her home, the fountainhead of maternal care, while looking to her husband to complement her worthy attributes by providing stability, security, support and firm direction.

A woman feels the need for this type of masculine stability even before she is married, and she responds to it when she encounters it in a way that resonates with her. In fact, when she meets a man with this type of firm assurance, she will be prepared to forego some of her preconceived notions for the sake of an excellent marriage.

When my friend in Argentina called up the reluctant young woman and spoke to her with sweet, gracious but firm assurance, she found this quality so appealing that she was willing to see him again. After all, she had really enjoyed his company when they had met. It was only his insistence on her covering her hair that had put her off. However, when she also saw in him the quality of male firmness in a gracious manner, the prospect of covering her hair did not seem dreadful enough to compel her to turn him down.

Someone once asked a great Mussar luminary which qualities he should seek in a prospective son-in-law.

He replied, "The Torah speaks of a father saying, 'I gave my daughter to this man.' It seems that the first requirement is that he be a man!"

A man.

What is a man? What masculine qualities entitle someone to be called a man in the fullest sense of the word?

In the Spanish language, special gender words are used for describing animals. A male animal is called *macho* and a female is called *hembra*. The word *macho* is also applied to a man in the sense of his having strong animalistic qualities. A man who is *macho* is considered strong, fearsome and domineering. Such a man can easily feel a sense of superiority over his wife, and he is likely to abuse her emotionally without even realizing that he is doing so. Such a man is likely to say, in effect, "I am the man of the house, and whatever I say, goes. No one is going to tell me what to do!"

But this is not how a man is defined according to the Torah. Before his passing, David HaMelech instructed Shlomo, his son and successor, to "be a man." *Targum* translates these words as an exhortation to Shlomo to fear the Lord and to recoil from sin. Manhood means strength, and the greatest strength is the ability to overcome the *yetzer hara*, the evil inclination. This is the manhood for which a Jewish woman yearns. This is the kind of firmness and stability she seeks to complement her own Jewish qualities.

David HaMelech advised his son Shlomo on how to be a wise ruler. He said (*II Shmuel* 23:3), "*Tzaddik moshel beyiras Elokim*. The righteous rule through fear of the Lord." A ruler who imposes his own will and desires on his subjects is a tyrant. A Jewish ruler is one who raises up the level of the people and brings them closer to fear of the Lord. A Jewish leader awakens the heart and inspires the soul; he does not twist the arm.

The quality of manhood that makes for a good Jewish husband is the ability to head a Jewish household with wisdom, sensitivity and a firm guiding hand so that it can become a sanctified resting place for the Divine Presence. When a husband is not focused on personal power, when he does not use his authority to impose his will on his household, when he cares deeply about reaching higher goals for the entire family, he will be sensitive to the needs and feelings of his wife. He will use his wisdom to seek out the route that will best bring his family closer to the Creator, and he will use his firmness and decisiveness to guide them along that route. This is the type of man for whom a Jewish woman yearns.

It is important for every Jewish husband to understand this. Even you, my son, who are so happily married and who has never seen the negative type of male behavior in the home of your parents, even you must be aware of the darker side of human nature in order to avoid it, in all circumstances and under all conditions. You must understand clearly the responsibilities of the leadership role that devolves upon you as the man of the house, and you must accept them upon yourself with humility and trepidation. Tread carefully, my son.

Let me tell you about a couple who decided to get divorced. Before preparing the *get*, the rabbi sent them to me for a last-minute attempt at reconciliation. The rabbi also sent me a list the wife had compiled, of her six most important complaints about her husband. This was such an amazing document that I never threw it away; I still have it in my possession. At the top of her list, she accused him of major abuse, although she declined to go into detail. The second complaint on the list was, "He doesn't like my friend Rose."

He doesn't like my friend Rose? Surely, this was no more than a trivial matter! Does it sound like a reason for a wife to demand a divorce from her husband? It made no sense.

I thought about it and thought about it, and then I understood. The Mishnah tells us that every person is a complete world unto himself. He must also feel that the whole world was created for him. In other words, the value of each individual human being is without measure. This awareness and these feelings play themselves out differently in every heart and soul, but they all have in common a tremendous sense of self-worth, of a self-image as an entire living, breathing, self-contained world.

This self-awareness in a married woman, however, is essentially precarious. On the one hand, she is her own complete world, but at the same time, she is also dependent on the leadership of her husband. If her husband abuses his position and power, if he treats her without sensitivity, understanding and tact, he can damage her sense of self-worth, and destroy her emotionally. Such abuse can be far more painful than physical abuse, because her whole sense of self is destroyed, and she feels worthless.

When this woman complained that her husband "doesn't like my friend Rose," she was subconsciously complaining about the emotional destruction her husband had inflicted on her. She could no longer be herself; she no longer saw herself as a separate and complete world, if her husband had to approve of her friends.

Consider this point in the context of a fairly commonplace scenario. A woman goes shopping for clothes for her children. She finds some things she really likes. They are really very expensive, but she likes them so much that she buys them anyway. She comes home, and her husband sees the bill. He has to sit down to catch his breath.

So what does he do?

The wise husband will sit down with his wife to discuss the issue patiently and in a non-confrontational, non-threatening, non-accusetory manner. He will describe the general financial situation of the family, and the kind of budget that will allow them to make ends meet. He will acknowledge that the clothes are beautiful and that nothing is too good for their children, but he will ask her gently to suggest how such clothes can fit into the budget at this particular time. If she has suggestions for some budget adjustments, he will listen to them with an open mind. After all, perhaps she is right. If it should turn out, however, that the clothes really do not fit into the family budget, his wife will understand perfectly, and she will admire him for his level-headedness and the firm exercise of his leadership responsibilities. She will look up to him as a man.

The *macho* husband, however, feels that he has to gain control of this madness before the family goes bankrupt. He takes possession of the checkbook and supervises every penny spent. Without realizing it, he crushes her beautiful world as a mother. She bought the clothes as an expression of her blossoming inner feelings of motherhood, and now she finds herself being controlled. She feels, as one woman once remarked to me, as if "she is in Auschwitz." Her world has been shattered.

So what has this *macho* husband accomplished? Fool that he is, he has damaged and alienated his wife and turned his home from a corner of paradise into a house of horrors. It does not show strength to stomp on a beautiful crystal glass and shatter it. If anything, it shows weakness.

My dear son,

Let me tell about my recent experience with a young man whom I shall call David. If you knew David at all, you would never think of him as the sort to have problems in his marriage.

He is amiable, friendly and popular. At home, however, he was an abusive husband. His wife had been trying for a long time to get him to speak with someone about the home situation, but he consistently refused. Then things got so bad that he finally agreed to come to me.

Before we began our conversation, I read to him the statement of the *Meiri* in *Bava Basra* (98a), "At home, it is improper for any person to be domineering over his children and household members. Instead, he should treat them with humility, so that they should not consider him a stranger."

Immediately, David had a violent reaction. "What? Humility? Are you saying I should act humbly to my wife? You must be joking. I am the man of the house. When I come home for supper, I expect supper to be ready. It's the least a man can expect in his own home. Humility! Hah! What am I supposed to do? Maybe I should bend my head, clasp my hands together and say, 'My holy rebbetzin, please forgive me for interrupting your holy telephone conversation. Do you think it is possible that you could spare a minute from your busy schedule to prepare a bite for me to eat? Would you be so kind?' Is that what you expect me to do? Rabbi, I know you like to fill the heads of the boys with beautiful Torah thoughts, but I am a man. If we're going to talk, we need to stay in the real world."

So what do you think, my son? Quite a frightening fellow under the surface, wouldn't you say? But at least we were off to a good start.

"Could I ask you a hypothetical question?" I said.

"Sure, Rabbi. Go right ahead."

"Imagine your own sister married a fellow who later became a robber and also abused her physically. What would you do?"

"Simple," he said. "I would kidnap her and whisk her away from that living hell. I can't imagine that anyone would do otherwise."

"You think that there is no other way, because you know of no other way. But the Sages disagreed. The Midrash tells (*Bereishis Rabbah* 20:3) about a woman from a distinguished family who married a robber who caused her suffering. The Sages, intending to rebuke him for his conduct, went to consult with her first. She said nothing about her home situation. Instead, she went into another room and returned with a golden candelabrum and an earthenware lamp perched upon it. The reason — "

"You know, Rabbi," David interrupted me, "it is really amazing that the Sages would go to the house of a robber to help straighten things out. They didn't give up on anyone!"

"Exactly right," I said. "They had faith in the essential goodness of every Jew, even a lowly robber. And did you notice that they were not coming to kidnap her, as you would have done? They were looking to improve the home situation, to alleviate the problems and bring husband and wife together."

"So if he was the problem, why didn't they go to him?"

"Good question. This shows the wisdom of the Sages. Before they could talk to him, they gauged her feelings about the situation. They understood that her perspective might be different from theirs. So they asked her about the situation, and she answered them in a roundabout way. She showed them the golden candelabrum, which symbolized her lineage, and she placed upon it the earthenware lamp, which symbolized her husband and his lowly station. And by placing one atop the other, she showed that they were, nonetheless, one. In other words, she still loved him dearly."

"So what happened? Did they speak to him? What did they say?"

"I don't know, David. The Midrash doesn't say. Another interesting thing that the Midrash doesn't tell us is how the robber managed to keep his wife's love for him alive. Doesn't that intrigue you?"

David fidgeted a little. "I suppose."

"I'll tell you something else though," I said. "Our Sages did tell us how a husband can destroy his wife's love. The statement of the *Meiri* that I quoted to you before, the one that upset you so much, pertains to a statement of the Gemara that 'an arrogant person is not accepted by his family.' The *Meiri* clarifies this by saying that a person who is less than humble at home is rejected by his family."

"What does arrogance have to do with rejection?"

"What is arrogance? It is assuming an exaggerated importance for yourself. The man of the house naturally wants to exercise authority, and in order to do so, he may assume an arrogant stance in order to control his family members. Very often, he may even resort to putting them down and damaging their self-esteem, in order to build himself up. This is the road to domestic disaster. He will alienate his family and become a stranger to them. In the end, he defeats his own purpose. He undermines his own authority, because no one wants to listen to a stranger. Instead of gaining control of his household, he loses control. So, he tries to assert himself even more, driving his family even further away. It is a downward spiral leading to tragedy."

I fixed him with a sharp stare.

"Do you know what I mean, David?" I said.

He avoided my eyes. "I – I'm not really sure. I think so." He took a deep breath and looked up at me. "Tell me, Rabbi, do I look like an arrogant person to you? Do you think my friends consider me arrogant?"

"I don't really know," I said. "It is quite possible that you do not come across as an arrogant person to your friends — but that doesn't prove anything. Sometimes, a man can act in a very acceptable manner in public but, in his own home, he needs to reinforce his self-image as a man. Where does that self-image come from? The gentile world, of course. The *macho* image portrayed in the media — the animalistic man. So he has to intimidate his wife and children by treating them as his servants. Perhaps his arrogance in the domestic setting may be his way of compensating for his own feelings of insecurity and inadequacy. He might see certain talents and virtues in his wife that he himself lacks, and he feels compelled to compensate by intimidating her. Does any of this sound familiar?"

He looked away. "I don't know," he said, "but I'm listening."

"My dear David," I continued, "you reacted violently before, when I spoke about humility. You don't seem to care for being humble. Well, I think you don't understand the meaning of humility. The Creator is called humble, because He showers everyone with goodness, even the undeserving. He is also called humble because He attaches value to all His creatures. I think you could be humble in the same way. Shower your wife with goodness even when she makes mistakes, showing her that she is important, while building up her self-esteem. Do you understand what you will accomplish? You will no longer be a domineering stranger in your own home. Your family will feel close to you, and this feeling of closeness will make you happy. You will then become a real man, in the Jewish sense, a man who gives guidance and direction to his family in kind and gentle terms, a man whose leadership and wisdom are willingly accepted."

David sighed and lowered his head. He sat quietly for a while, then he looked up. He seemed to have undergone an inner change.

"So, Rabbi," he said, "do you think I can change?"

"Why not?" I replied. "If the Sages thought they could get a robber to change, I think you should certainly be able to straighten things out with your wife. As you say, though, the change has to be in you. Yes, David, I think you can change."

By the way, David did change. Last I heard, things were going well for him at home.

You know, my son, the *Meiri* was not only talking to people like David, extreme cases of domestic arrogance. He was speaking to "any person," even people like you and me, who are happily married. We also have to be extremely careful to be humble in our relationships with our wives.

The *Reishis Chachmah* writes that a man should be more humble with his wife than with other people. Since his dealings with other people usually take place in public in full view of his friends and associates, he is unlikely to be haughty and behave in an inappropriate way. His shame and fear of public disapproval will ensure that he remains kind, polite and patient. On the other hand, his relationship with his wife is conducted in private, unrestrained by public opinion. There is nothing to stop him from becoming arrogant and domineering. Therefore, it is important that he make a special effort to be humble in his relationship with his wife.

A friend of mine once told about a disagreement he had with his wife regarding a question of some importance. The door was open, since they were waiting for a taxi to take them to a family affair at which they would be meeting an associate of theirs. While they waited for the taxi, they argued about how to deal with this person. The husband was getting very frustrated with his wife's refusal to accept his point of view. He felt she was being unreasonable and unrealistic but, despite all the arguments he offered, he could not get her to change her mind. He was on the verge of asserting himself in a rather negative way, when he looked up and saw the taxi driver standing in the doorway.

"The minute I saw the driver," my friend said to me, "my personality changed. My blood cooled, and my breathing returned to normal. I went over to my wife and pressed my argument in as soft a manner as I could. And guess what? She saw that I was right. Can you imagine?"

∽

My dear son,

I wanted to add a short postscript to the previous letter. No, it is not a story about my childhood in Argentina. It is just some simple advice about how to develop the virtue of humility in your relationship with your wife.

When Miriam was afflicted with *tzaraas*, Moshe said a brief prayer for her. Rashi tells us that Moshe kept it brief so that the Jewish people would not say, "His sister is suffering, and he is saying long prayers." There is much to discuss about this Rashi, but not right now. The bottom line is that Moshe kept his prayer to a minimum — only five words! And one of these words was "please."

"Please" is a critical word. It changes the entire complexion of a statement. When a person say "please," he indicates that he is asking for a favor. He acknowledges that the other person is not obligated to do it — that he would only be doing it out of the kindness of his heart. When a person doesn't say "please," he is issuing a command. It is as if he is punching a key on the computer, which has no choice but to obey his command. He is treating the other person as his computer.

A person issues a check when he has money in the bank. If he has no money in his account, he makes an application for a loan. He absolutely does not write out a check with the arrogant expectation that the bank will honor it. He says "please" and hopes the bank will say "okay."

My dear son, you have always been a polite young man. When you speak to your wife, politeness is very important, but it is not enough. You have to remember that one magic word. Please. It will show your respect, fortify her self-esteem and make your marriage a never-ending joy.

My dear son,

A funny thing happened last week. Or maybe it wasn't so funny. But it all turned out well.

Our little neighbor Nuchem was learning in school about Yehudah HaMacabee, and his *rebbe* was giving the boys quite a graphic presentation. He swung his ruler over his head like a sword and stormed the imaginary Greeks. Well, Nuchem's imagination was all fired up, and when he came home he decided to be Yehudah HaMacabee as well. Only he didn't use a ruler as his make-believe sword. He used a long, sharp carving knife from the kitchen drawer.

His father heard the screaming and came out to the sight of Nuchem charging around the living room brandishing his "sword" over his head and slashing through the air in front of him. His father asked Nuchem to put down the knife, but Nuchem was not prepared to surrender so easily. After all, the fate of the Jewish people was in his hands. This went on for a harrowing few minutes, until he finally agreed to disarm. I'm not quite sure what inducement his father offered him, but it worked.

Now tell me, my son, during those hair-raising minutes that Nuchem held the knife, was he his father's enemy? Of course not. It was just a dangerous situation that had to be handled with wisdom and defused.

The same applies to most confrontations between husband and wife. Regardless of how strongly, shrilly and vehemently one may confront the other, it is not a sign of enmity. At least not in the beginning. The proper response is to defuse the situation, not to counterattack with maximum force. You do not want to turn a domestic confrontation into a war.

I once visited a city to attend a wedding, and the local rabbi asked me to speak with a certain lawyer. The man was erudite, gracious and considerate in public, but at home he was an abusive tyrant. He refused to discuss his domestic situation with anyone, but something had to be done, and the rabbi asked me to speak to the man. My mission was to discover his problem and to deliver the remedy without his realizing what I was doing. Quite a tall order!

The rabbi arranged for the lawyer to be seated next to me at the wedding, and we got into a long conversation. He was a pleasant fellow, and I really enjoyed talking to him. After a while, I began to tell him stories about my attempts to solve marital problems. He listened with interest and asked many questions, especially about dealing with strong-minded women. I realized that he saw his wife as an adversary, and that his abusiveness was his way of defending himself. So I steered the discussion in that direction and told him stories about those types of marital disputes.

The lawyer became very excited. "Rabbi, I thought you were a *Mashgiach*," he said. "Are you also a psychologist? Are you an expert at family therapy?"

I was about to give my standard reply that I had learned my psychology from Rabbeinu Yonah, whom the Alter of Kelm described as the Master Psychologist – but then I had another idea.

"Actually, I do have some expertise in therapy," I said. "I am trained in the Billiken Method."

"I knew it! It is obvious that you are a professional psychologist, but what is this Billiken Method? I can't say I've ever heard of it. Can you tell me something about it?"

"Of course," I said. "I'm not surprised that you never heard of the Billiken Method, because I studied it in Buenos Aires. You see, when my parents came to Argentina from Germany they were penniless and life was a struggle. You cannot imagine the hardships they encountered just to put food on the table, but they made sure that the children would not be affected by the hardships. We never felt deprived, and our house was always full of joy. They were also very careful not to have any disagreements in front of the children. I cannot say if they ever argued or disagreed in private, but I can say that I never saw anything of the sort. Growing up, I used to think that all parents were just like mine, that they always spoke nicely to each other, and that they always loved their children and loved each other. This created quite a problem for me."

The lawyer looked at me quizzically. "A problem? This is a problem? I should have such problems, and so should everyone else."

I smiled. "Oh, it wasn't a personal problem. For me, everything was wonderful, but how was I to help others with marital problems if I could not relate to them on a personal level?"

"Ah, I see what you mean. How would you understand the feelings of couples that fight when you never even knew such a thing existed?"

"Exactly,"

"Okay, that is a problem. So what did you do?"

"I used the Billiken Method."

"So at last we come to this mysterious method. What is it?"

"*Billiken* was a weekly scholastic publication for schoolchildren in Argentina, something like *Highlights* in the United States. Every issue had a page of comic strips that were quite popular. They made a powerful impression on me. In fact, I still remember some of them. In one of these strips a stout lady carrying a stick in one hand and a rolling pin in the other was always putting her husband in his place. Week in and week out, these two were back at it again."

The lawyer laughed.

"You understand, don't you?" I said gently. "The Billiken Method taught me that there are different wives and different husbands and that some couples play out their relationships in rather strange ways. One thing I have learned over the years is that a wife who is strong-minded and assertive is not her husband's enemy. However, if he perceives her as his enemy, there is bound to be trouble. If he thinks he has to mobilize his reserves and pulverize her, there is no chance for their marriage. If he would only try to calm her down and mollify her, instead of mounting a counterattack, he would be surprised at how quickly the situation would be defused."

— *6* —

Respect Your Wife

My dear son,

Everyone is taught that Columbus discovered America, but someone else actually caught the first glimpse of the New World. It was the lookout in the crow's nest high up on the mast. He was the first to see the dark outline on the horizon. "*Tierra!*" he called out. "Land!" This sailor knew he had sighted land, but he had no idea he had sighted a continent.

When you begin to explore the topic of respecting your wife, you are like that sailor who discovered America. You read the words of the Talmud (*Yevamos* 62b) that praise a husband who is "*mechabdah yoseir migufo,*" who respects his wife more than himself. You know you are seeing the requirement of a proper standard of behavior toward your wife. You see clearly that a man must be respectful to his wife, but you do not yet realize how vast and important this topic really is. You do not yet appreciate the depth and beauty of this respect. It is like a continent.

First of all, we need to distinguish between good manners, which is a superficial virtue, and respect, which is virtue rooted deep in the heart, soul and intellect.

There is a famous story about a student in the Slobodka Yeshivah who visited Germany and came back very impressed with the civility of the people. Whenever people gave him directions, they would add politely, "*Nicht wahr?* Isn't that so?" He found this politeness so charming that he praised the German people highly upon his return to the yeshivah. The wiser heads in the yeshivah pointed out to him that he was confusing external manners with inner refinement, but he would not hear of it. He was convinced that Germans were the finest people.

Years later, he was deported to Auschwitz. Dr. Mengele, the infamous Nazi, chose him for some of his grisly experiments to determine the human tolerance level for pain. He kept submitting the young man to all sorts of torture, and every time, he would say to him gently, "It hurts, *nicht wahr?* It hurts, *nicht wahr?*" Unfortunately, the young man had to learn the difference between politeness and respect the hard way.

The Torah tells us (*Bereishis* 12:8) that Avraham "moved from there to the mountain . . . and he pitched his tent (*ahalo*) . . . and he built there an altar to God." Rabbeinu Bachya writes that the Kabbalistic significance of Avraham's "moving to the mountain," which was Mount Moriah, was that he reached great mystical heights in his inner thoughts. This was not a simple journey into the mountains. It was the heroic scaling of soaring mystical mountains — the penetration to the deepest secrets of Creation.

The altar Avraham built in Mount Moriah was undoubtedly a crucial element in his mystical ascent but, before he built the altar, he pitched his tent. The masculine possessive *ahalo*, his tent, ordinarily ends with the letter *vav* but, in this case, it ends with the letter *heh*, as in the spelling of the feminine possessive.

The commentators explain that, although it is read as *ahalo* — his tent, the spelling indicates that he actually built *ahalah*, her tent, immediately upon his arrival in Mount Moriah — even before he built the altar. Why? Because "a man must respect his wife more than he does himself." In the midst of describing this exalted moment in Avraham's spiritual development, the Torah informs all future generations of the crucial importance of showing respect to one's wife.

Avraham could never have attained his spiritual accomplishments, nor could he have discovered his mystical secrets, if had not shown Sarah such great respect. He would have been a lesser man. The respect he showed to his wife underscored the purity of his *tzelem Elokim*, his bearing of the flawless image of the Lord, in which man was created. A person can behave in a certain manner in public, but "let loose" when he retires to the privacy of his home. By conducting himself with respect toward his wife in the privacy of his home, he showed himself for the great person he was. By pitching her tent first, he gave priority to her needs over his and showed her great respect. Her pressing need for modesty also led Avraham to pitch his wife's tent first. Once again, by giving priority to her need for modesty, he showed his wife great respect, and this itself enabled him to attain his spiritual elevation.

I once traveled with R' Nosson Wachtfogel *zt"l*, the Mashgiach of the Lakewood Yeshivah, to raise funds for the Yeshivah. His saintly appearance attracted many people, many of whom attempted to show themselves as dedicated servants of the Creator. One fellow in particular stood out, but I later discovered that it was all superficial. When I got to know him better, I saw that he was not exactly a person who feared Heaven, to say the least. Years later, this man confessed to me that he treated his wife shabbily in private — even being abusive to her. I was not surprised.

Now, I cannot tell you for certain if his lack of *yiras shamayim* led him to be abusive or if his abusive behavior prevented him from developing his *yiras shamayim,* but this I can tell you, for certain: If you want your home to be a dwelling place for the Divine Presence, if you want happiness, joy and holiness to reign supreme in your home, heed the words of our Sages and respect your wife more than you do yourself.

My dear son,

Respect your wife more than yourself. Such an interesting concept. The insight of the Sages is really quite amazing. I don't think a secular person could understand this concept. Why should you respect your wife more than you respect yourself? Is it fair?

The *Raavad* explains it with an incisive analogy. A man generally takes care of his body without giving preference to any one of its limbs or parts. They are all precious and equal to him. You will never hear someone say, "I've got to take care of my eyes, but I really couldn't be bothered about my toes." When he goes outside in the freezing cold, he will cover certain body parts more readily than others. He will usually leave his face exposed but make sure that his feet are well insulated and protected. Why is this so? Are his feet more precious to him than his eyes and his nose? Hardly. It is because the parts of his body sensitive to cold need to be covered well, while the parts resistant to cold can be left exposed.

Husband and wife are like one body, with every individual part precious to the whole. The husband sees to his wife's needs just as he sees to his own, because his wife's needs are indeed his own. Nonetheless, there are some parts of this composite whole, this husband and wife combination, that are more sensitive and need more care than others.

When it comes to issues of respect, the wife is usually more sensitive than the husband. Therefore, the husband must deliver more respect to his wife, who is the sensitive part of the whole. When a husband goes out of his way to give his wife more respect than he seeks for himself, his extreme sensitivity to her concerns and needs gives her a sense of stability, security and self-worth. When a husband feels his wife's needs as acutely as he does his own, he will fulfill them to the best of his ability, regardless of the interference with his busy schedule or other inconvenience. This is a path that leads directly to marital peace and marital bliss.

Have you lost patience yet with my little stories about my life in Argentina? No? Good, because here is another one.

While I was in Buenos Aires, I was asked to substitute for a few weeks for a class of young boys were just beginning to learn *Rashi*. I was also warned about one particular youngster who was a terror in the classroom. As you would expect, it did not take more than five minutes for this little troublemaker to turn the class upside down with his antics. He seemed like a nice boy, but I could tell that something was bothering him.

I called him over during the break and said, "I know what you're up to. You want to show me that you're the worst boy in the class, but I have news for you. You can't fool me. You are a sweet, wonderful Jewish child, and nothing you can do will convince me otherwise."

Do you know what happened? From that moment on, he was the best behaved child in the class — an absolute angel. What made him respond this way? The love I had shown him certainly helped, but it was more than that. Had I shown him love in other ways, it would not have been as effective. However, what I said to him showed that I understood him, that I was aware of his inner turmoil, and that I was concerned about it. I showed him that I believed in him, and that I trusted in his good side. This is why he responded so positively.

It is the same in the relations between husband and wife, at home. When Avraham showed Sarah that he was sensitive to her needs, that she needed her tent immediately for reasons of modesty, he showed her that he understood and was sensitive to her. Such sensitivity opens wide the gates of love and marital bliss.

Listen, my son, to the words of your father. Build your home on the foundation of this advice of our Sages. Respect your wife more than yourself, and your home will always be filled with love, peace and joy.

$\backsim$

My dear son,

There was once an earthquake in Eretz Yisrael during R' Yosef Chaim Sonenfeld's later years, when he was already feeble and infirm. As soon as the tremor passed, his grandson ran to his room and found him sitting over the Gemara, as if nothing had happened.

When he heard the boy come in, R' Yosef Chaim looked up and said very calmly, "Did you make the *berachah* over an earthquake yet?"

The boy nodded.

"Good," said his grandfather. "Now go back to your learning."

This is not exactly how you would expect a person to react to an earthquake. People who experience an earthquake are generally so upset that it takes them a long time to get back to functioning normally. How, then, did R' Yosef Chaim maintain his composure?

A child is terrified when he faces danger, but he feels better if he is holding his father's hand — even if his father is not capable of protecting him. Why is this so? Because fear is an emotional, rather than a logical, reaction. When a child holds his father's hand, he feels an intrinsic sense of security that allows him to face the danger without an overly emotional reaction. A woman is at home during a thunderstorm and feels frightened. Her husband calls her on the telephone and speaks with her for a few minutes, and she feels better after she hangs up. Did that conversation give her any added protection against the crashing thunder and lightning? Of course not. But the contact with her husband reinforced her sense of security and allowed her to endure the horrendous noises of the thunderstorm without any undue emotional reaction.

The ground shaking and trembling under your feet is so emotionally disturbing that you completely lose your sense of security. R' Yosef Chaim derived his security from his contact with the Gemara that he held in his hands, and the earthquake did not upset his emotional equilibrium.

A married woman needs to feel secure in her marriage and her relationship with her husband. It is an important emotional need. Our Sages addressed this need by instituting the *kesubah*, which guarantees her financial and emotional security. One of the promises in the *kesubah* is *ve'okir*, and I will esteem. Some commentators see this as the husband's promise to respect her more than he does himself. This powerful respect and sensitivity are the mainstays of her security in her marriage.

The Midrash (*Eichah Rabbah* 3:19) tells of a king who married a noblewoman and wrote her a generous *kesubah*. One day, the king set out on an ocean voyage, and he was not heard from for a very long time. His wife waited patiently for his return, but as the time wore on without any word from him, her friends and neighbors mocked her. "The king has abandoned you," they said. "He will never come back to you." She broke down in tears and ran into her house. She went to the place where she kept her important papers and took out the *kesubah*. As she read through the long document, a feeling of peace came over her and she was comforted.

When the king finally returned, he was amazed to find his wife patiently awaiting his return. "Tell me, my dear wife," he said, "how did you manage to wait for me without despairing for all these years?"

"It was the generous *kesubah* you gave me," she replied. "If not for that, I would have given up a long time ago."

What do you think she was saying, my son? How did the generous *kesubah* keep her spirits up? If he meant to abandon her, a generous *kesubah* would not have made him change his mind. He would not have honored it.

The answer is that when the wife reads her *kesubah*, when she recalls the commitments and the promises her husband made to her on their wedding day, she feels a new security in his love for her. When this noblewoman read the generous *kesubah* that her husband had given her, she felt such a sense of his powerful love for her that she was convinced that it would endure forever. With such a love in his heart, his failure to return could only have been caused by unavoidable delays and obstacles. She felt sure that the love burning in his heart would eventually lead him back to her.

The Chazon Ish writes that a wife's dependency on her husband for his care, attention and concern becomes part of her very being. Just as firm ground under our feet give us a sense of security, so does her husband's support give her a sense of security. Just as a brief earth tremor can throw a person into a panic, a husband's insensitivity and indifference can cause panic in the innermost chambers of her heart.

A well-known *rosh yeshivah* was telling me about a young couple that had an argument. In the heat of the exchange, the husband said, "You know, I really could do without you."

I observed that this was a particularly nasty remark, the exact opposite of "respect your wife more than yourself" — a thrust that undermined her security.

The *rosh yeshivah* shook his head. "It was much more than that. This foolish husband caused the same commotion in his wife's soul that handing her a *get* would have caused. He rocked the ground under her feet."

My son, a person needs to feel secure in order to function, to live. A person who feels insecure and unstable cannot lead a productive and successful life. So you see, you hold your wife's very life in your power. If you treat her properly, if you respect her more than yourself, she will feel a strong sense of security. She will blossom and flourish and fill your life with happiness and joy.

⌒

My dear son,

While we are still on the subject of respect for your wife, I would like to discuss the issue of how you should speak to her and how you should address her. The things you say, the words you choose and the manner in which you speak can be devastating.

You were always a polite boy, but it is far from uncommon for young boys to speak roughly to each other, especially to those who appear weak to them. I wince when I hear them speak to each other, but what can I do? Can I change the world? I console myself with the thought that one day these immature boys will grow up and become sensitive, caring adults. I hope.

As you know, the boys in yeshivah can be brutally frank with each other on Purim. Many things they would not dare say all year come flowing out as the wine flows in.

Well, let me tell about one of the students in the yeshivah, many years ago. This fellow was a real braggart. He never stopped talking about himself, his talents, his contacts, his money and his accomplishments. The other students considered him an obnoxious and generally odious person. One Purim, they decided to put him in his place. After they had all had a little to drink, they "let him have it" and really "put him in his place," if you know what I mean. The very next day, the student suffered a nervous breakdown.

The students who "put him in his place" felt that a few harsh words would make him see the light, but look at what happened. They only succeeded in destroying his self-esteem and self-image and in erasing the emotional support that he needed in order to function. The result was a nervous breakdown. Look how dangerous words can be.

My son, your wife, being a woman and a married one (no less), is intrinsically more sensitive than that student, although she is probably more stable. You have to speak gently and kindly to your wife, always bolstering her self-esteem and security and never undermining them. You cannot talk to her with the rough language and harsh manner you might consider when talking to a man. In fact, you should never even talk that way to anyone at all.

The Talmud tells us (*Gittin* 52a) that R' Yosi used to call his wife *beisi*, my home. When we give our loved ones affectionate names, we show what they mean to us. A mother will call her children sweetheart, because they are sweet on her heart. R' Yosi called his wife *beisi*, because, to him, she was the embodiment of that precious thing called home. Every person needs a home; otherwise he is a piece of driftwood. It is more than a luxury, even more than a necessity. It is an essential part of being human. R' Yosi saw in his wife the complete fulfillment of home. She was his home. She was his life. By calling her *beisi*, he gave her respect and the ultimate appreciation of what she meant to him.

Marriage is a long road, and there inevitably are rough stretches. Remember, my son, that your wife is your home, the very essence of your life, and you will get through the hard times without damaging your relationship. Speak to her kindly and respectfully, and you will be happy for the rest of your life.

My dear son,

We've been discussing all along the Talmud's statement that a man should "respect his wife more than himself," but that is only part of it. The complete text is *"Ohavah kegufo umechabdah yoseir migufo. He loves her as he loves himself, and he respects her more than he respects himself." These are two different things. Certain things he does for her out of love. For these, he should exert himself for her as much as he would exert himself for his own needs. Other things he does for her out of respect. For these, he should set a higher standard for her than he sets for himself.

We'll get into this a little more deeply in a minute. First, I want to tell you a story I read in the journal *Yeshurun*. It is told about the Vilna Gaon, although I cannot guarantee its authenticity.

The Gaon's travels took him to the city of Amsterdam, where he was invited to stay in the home of a very wealthy man. The Gaon was exhausted, and he welcomed a few days of rest before continuing on his journey. The wealthy man took a liking to the

Gaon and invited him to stay as long as he wished. The Gaon accepted gratefully, because he found it comfortable and convenient in the man's home, especially because there was a *minyan* in the vicinity three times a day.

The Gaon stayed there three weeks, and then, thoroughly refreshed, he took his leave of his host. The host parted with him with great reluctance, and escorted him from his home with pomp and fanfare. As the wagon was about to leave, the wealthy man stepped forward for one last word with the Gaon.

"Over the last three weeks," he said, "I have become convinced that you are one of the great scholars of the Jewish people. I have seen how you conducted yourself and how you spent all your time learning. So if you don't mind, I would like your advice. You have also had the opportunity to observe me and my household. Do you approve of what you have seen? Is there anything you would have me change?"

"Heaven forbid," said the Gaon. "You have a beautiful home. May the Almighty give you the strength to continue in this way forever. However, since you ask, I will mention one thing. Our Sages speak about a man who loves his wife as he loves himself. That means it should be the same and not more. A man's respect for his wife should exceed his respect for himself but, with regard to love, they should be the same. This is the Talmud's guideline. In your home, I saw something else. I saw you bring her water to wash her hands. I saw you bring her coffee to her bedroom, when you yourself do not even drink coffee! This is the only flaw I noticed."

"Let me explain," said the man. "It goes back to my childhood. I come from a distinguished family, and my father was a well-known *talmid chacham* — but he was not a wealthy man. When I was nine years old, my father arranged a match for me with the nine-year-old daughter of a wealthy man who lived not far from our town. The marriage would take place when we reached the age of fifteen. My prospective father-in-law agreed to give his daughter a handsome dowry and to support us. In the meantime, he paid for my clothes and shoes, and he hired a private tutor for me. I made great progress in my learning during those years.

"Just when I was turning fifteen, my prospective father-in-law's fortunes took a turn for the worse, unknown to us, and he basically lost his money. When the date set for the marriage drew closer, my father went to see him and discuss his commitments to me. He admitted that he could not fulfill them, and the engagement was broken.

"A short while later, I became engaged to the daughter of another wealthy man who lived in a nearby village. We were married, and not long afterward, I fell ill. My father-in-law spent a lot of money on doctors and medicines, but it was all to no avail. Seeing no hope for my recovery, my father-in-law sent me off to the communal poorhouse. I lay there in my sickbed, getting worse and worse every day. My father-in-law came and asked me to give a *get* to my wife, which I consented to do. Eventually, my condition stabilized, but I was still sickly and debilitated, barely able to walk under my own power.

"One day, a beggar came over to me in the poorhouse and said, 'It is obvious that you are a *talmid chacham* and that you are extremely poor. I would like to make a proposal. You and I will form a team. I will rent a wagon and transport you from village to village. You will answer people's questions, and they will give us money.'

"I agreed, and this is what we did. We used to come to a town with me lying in the wagon too weak to walk on my own power. I would explain a difficult *Tosafos* or a piece of *Maharsha* to the people, and they would give us more money than they gave the other beggars. We did rather well for ourselves, considering our situation.

"One day, we came across another beggar who was doing virtually the same thing we were. He was transporting his daughter in a wagon; she was also apparently too weak to walk on her own power. He went from house to house, and people took pity on his stricken daughter and gave generously.

"At my partner's urging, we made a broader partnership. We both went collecting with our respective wagons, and at the end of the day, we would pool our earnings and divide them equally. It was a good arrangement, and it worked out well.

"After a while, it only seemed natural that the daughter and I should get married, even though we were both exceedingly infirm. We had a very small, private wedding. After the *chupah*, my new bride began to cry bitterly.

"'Why are you crying?' I said.

"'How can I not cry?' she lamented. 'My father used to be a rich man. When I was nine years old, he selected for me an exceptional boy from a distinguished family. He took care of the boy for five years, dressing him and buying him shoes. Then my father lost his money, and the engagement was broken. Now look how far I've fallen. I am still young, but I am as sickly and feeble as an old woman, and I am being married to a beggar who is as sick and feeble as I am. And who knows what kind of family you are from? Don't get me wrong. You are a good man, but look how far I have fallen. Look what has become of me.'

"I was shocked when I heard these words, because she was clearly speaking about me. I told her who I was and that she was my first bride. At first, she was incredulous, but after we spoke for a while, she saw that it was true. We were both overjoyed to have found each other again.

"Our fortunes turned, right after we were married. We both returned to health, and we prospered. The Almighty helped us at every step of the way and blessed us with fine, upstanding sons and daughters.

"This, then, is my story. I know that I caused her years of anguish, and that anything I do for her will not be enough to erase my debt to her."

The Gaon nodded gravely. "In that case," he said, "you should continue to do as you have been doing."

He delayed his journey in order to spend two more days with his host, and he gave special blessings to his children before he left.

This, my son, is the story, more or less, as it is quoted in *Yeshurun*. An incredible story, isn't it?

Before I read this story, I had a different understanding of the concept of *"ohavah kegufo,* loving a wife as one loves oneself." I understood this to be a minimum standard. You should exert yourself at least as much as you would exert yourself for your own needs. However, if you wanted to do more for your wife, do so by all means. With regard to respect, however, the minimum standard is to respect her more than yourself. This is how I understood it.

According to the Gaon, however, this is apparently wrong. You should not love her more than yourself. The standard of *ohavah kegufo* is equality, not less, not more. When the Gaon saw this man doing more for his wife than he would ever do for himself, he rebuked him for it. It was the only flaw he found in the man's household.

How do we understand this? Why shouldn't a person pamper his wife and give her more than he would take for himself?

Let me tell you what I think.

A father loves all his children equally. Why? Because they are his children. It is natural for fathers to love their children. Now, let us say that one of the children is a musical prodigy, and the father harbors a special love for this child. Would you say that this special love is a fatherly love? I would say that it is not. As far as fatherly love is concerned, one child does not differ from the other. The cause of fatherly love is the father-child connection, and in this connection, all children are equal. So, why does the father have a special love for his little musical prodigy? He is proud of the child. He takes a vicarious pleasure in the child's triumphs. And so on. These reasons give rise to a selfish love, not a fatherly love.

It is the same with husband and wife. The source of the love between them is that they were created for each other, that they are as one body, one organism. A person should love his wife because he believes and has faith that she and he are part of the same whole. Just as he cares for his arm or his eyes, he should care for her. But if he loves her more than himself, it is a sign that the love is rooted in something else, perhaps physical desire, perhaps something else. This is not the love the Torah mandates for husband and wife. Therefore, the Gaon frowned on his host's excessive solicitude to the needs of his wife.

Had we been in the home of that host and observed his conduct, we might have thought how nice it was for a husband to treat his wife so beautifully, or we might have thought that he was perhaps overdoing it a bit. The Gaon, however, with his sharp understanding of the words of our Sages, understood that he was doing something wrong.

So you see, my son, the love between husband and wife should be based on the solid bedrock of your recognition that you are both one, not on pleasures, emotions and desires. These things can change, allowing the love to evaporate. On the other hand, your preordained bond with each other will never change, and your love will endure and continue to grow forever.

As a child in Argentina — here I go with Argentina again! — I remember riding in a crowded bus and seeing an old man give his seat to a healthy young woman. What was the point? Believe me, he needed the seat more than she did. He was responding to his own natural desires, which made him favorably disposed to her. I assure you that if she had been plain and dowdy, he would not have offered her his seat. A husband's love for his wife should not be so superficial. It should be rooted in the profound bond that connects them.

This is what the Gaon said to his host, and the host replied that he treated her this way to make amends for all the years of pain she had suffered through him. In this case, of course, his behavior was perfectly justified.

Did you also notice in the story that, after the Gaon heard his host's explanation, he decided to stay on for another two days and bless his children? The Gaon was already being escorted out the door to his wagon. He had already turned to say his final good-bye, but when he heard the story, he went back into the house and stayed for two more days. Why?

I think it is because he was *chosheid bechaveiro*. He had unjustly suspected his host of improper behavior. Perhaps he felt that he should have asked him to explain himself before he rebuked him. In any case, he apparently felt obligated to apologize and make amends for offending his host, and he devoted two whole days to it.

There is another important lesson to be learned from this story. If a husband causes his wife great pain, there is practically no limit to the length he must go in order to make amends, just like the Gaon's host did. Even if he is guilty of a relatively minor offense against his wife, he does not get off with a simple "sorry." He should be especially nice to her for at least two days, don't you think?

My dear son,

I've told you a number of times about my friend who is a *rebbe* in a yeshivah. He always has interesting stories to tell, stories from which I derive insight into life in general, not only in the classroom.

Recently, he told me about a certain boy who always does poorly on his Gemara tests. So, you ask, what's surprising about that? There are some boys who have trouble with Gemara. True, but this boy was a mystery. You see, he was one of the best boys in the class. He listened well, studied hard and had a sharp mind. He should have excelled on his tests but, instead, he barely managed to pass. What was going on?

One day, the *rebbe* called the boy aside.

"You know," he said, "there's a major test tomorrow, don't you?"

"Yes, *rebbe*," the boy answered nervously.

"Well, are you prepared? Are you ready to take the test?"

"N-not really. Not yet."

"What's the problem?" asked the rebbe. "Did you learn . . .?"

The rebbe went on to mention different pieces of the Gemara, and for each piece, the boy said, "I know that one."

Finally, the rebbe mentioned a particularly difficult *Tosafos*.

"I don't know that one well yet, *rebbe*," the boy said. "I just review it and review, but I can't get it right."

"I'll tell you what," said the *rebbe*. "You are exempt from answering any questions on that *Tosafos* tomorrow. Just take care of all the rest, alright?"

The boy looked relieved. He nodded his head and ran off to join his friends.

The next day, the boy completed the entire test except for the question relating to that one *Tosafos*. And guess what? He got 100%!

So what do you say? This is one clever *rebbe*, isn't he? The *rebbe* understood that the boy was a perfectionist. As long as he did not know everything perfectly, he did not consider himself prepared. He brooded and worried until his whole peace of mind was destroyed and he could not handle any of the test, not even those parts that he knew very well.

Once the *rebbe* released him from answering questions relating to that difficult *Tosafos*, he relaxed and earned a perfect mark.

You see what an important lesson this is in life? When a person worries too much about a small detail, he can spoil everything for himself.

It is exactly the same in the relationship between husband and wife. The *Mesillas Yesharim* writes (22) that it is impossible for a person to be perfect. Even the most exalted person has numerous flaws, whether in his nature, his background or his experiences. Therefore, when a husband considers his wife, it is inevitable that he will notice some faults, but at the same time he sees all her wonderful qualities, the ones that convinced him to marry her, and her faults and shortcomings seem trivial by comparison.

Sometimes, however, a husband may come up against one of his wife's faults in certain situations, when he cannot simply overlook it. In that case, especially if he is a bit of a perfectionist, there is a real danger that he may become obsessed with that imperfection, and it begins to gnaw at him and gnaw at him. He begins to look at his wife as an inferior person, and he loses sight of all her wonderful qualities. If this is allowed to go on, it can literally undermine the marriage.

The first thing the husband must do in such a situation is focus on all her good qualities. He should think about them and remind himself of all the good she has always done for him. By doing so, he will come to the realization that whatever fault she has is only a small part of the entire person that she is, just like the one hard question is not the entire Gemara test. He has to come to the realization that this is simply an isolated problem that needs to be addressed.

When Moshe *Rabbeinu* went down to Egypt, the Jewish people, weary and distracted, did not listen to him right away. Moshe was upset, and Hashem told him to continue his mission, despite his temporary setback. Rashi explains that Hashem told Moshe to lead them gently and be forbearing of their shortcomings.

The *Zohar* gives us a broader view of what Hashem told Moshe. He said, "Speak to the Jewish people gently because, even though they are beset with hard labor, they are nonetheless princes, descendants of royalty. They did not betray their traditions nor did they assimilate with alien people. They stood their holy ground."

Listen to what Hashem was saying to Moshe. Although you have encountered them in a demeaning condition, and you have seen their faults, remember that they are royalty. Remember their great virtues. Remember that they held their holy ground despite all the hardship that they faced. Focus on their virtues and you will not be so disturbed by their faults.

That is one part of what Hashem said to Moshe. The second part was, "Speak gently to them." You want to be successful? You want your message to get through? You want to catch their attention and get them to listen? It will only work if you speak gently to them. Particularly because they are such a highborn people, you must speak to them with respect.

This is exactly how a husband should relate to his wife. See all her great virtues, focus on her goodness and wonderful qualities, so that the faults will not be blown out of proportion. And then speak to her gently, if you want to get your point across. In addition, keep in mind that if you want her to treat you like a king then you must treat her like a queen. Speak to her as you would speak to royalty, gently and with great respect.

My dear son,

Human nature is such that when a person is truly happy, he feels benevolent towards the people around him. When he is unhappy, he takes it out on the people around him.

What then, does it take to make a person happy? The *Maharal* writes that a person is happy when he feels a sense of completeness — when a certain void has been filled. It follows that true happiness comes only from *ruchnius*, from spiritual achievements. A person who reaches new heights in *ruchnius* gains a sense of fulfillment. It is, however, not the same with *gashmius*, material things. The Vilna Gaon says that the material world is like drinking salty water. The more you drink the thirstier you are. So where is happiness? When do you feel fulfilled? Never!

This, my son, is an important key to happiness in a marriage. A person who looks for spiritual fulfillment understands that his marriage has brought him innumerable benefits. He feels overflowing with happiness, and he thanks Hashem for all his blessings. He esteems and values his wife, looks at her in a positive light, and seeks to make her happy. The home will be filled with love, harmony and joy. If he is focused on material things, however, he will find true happiness a very elusive goal. He will be grumpy and bad-tempered. More likely than not, he will take it out on his wife, and the home will become a battleground.

Do you ever drive through an exact change toll booth and throw your coins into the bin? The sign lights up and says, "Toll paid. Thank you." How much emotion is there in that "thank you"? How much feeling and sincerity?

Of course, it is nice to put up such a sign. It shows a certain civility on the part of the toll people. That is a good thing, but each "thank you" is a robotic response, purely mechanical, with no feeling or warmth at all.

Well, the husband who is truly happy will thank his wife with warmth and deep sincerity, and she will feel honored, appreciated and ever so close to him. The unhappy husband will, at best, just go through the motions. If he says "thank you" it will be with the same measure of feeling as that sign in the toll booth.

One final point: You have to know how to ask for something properly. A poor man comes to a rich man and asks for a rather large loan. If he asks as if it is coming to him, he is unlikely to get it, but if he asks humbly, showing that he knows he has no right to it, he stand a much better chance of getting it.

It is the same between husband and wife. When a husband demands things because he feels it is coming to him, the natural reaction of the wife is to resist. On the other hand, if he asks with humility, showing that he knows he does not have it coming to him, his wife will feel an overwhelming desire to give him what he needs and make him happy. After all, he is the most important person in her life, the person to whom she feels most attached.

So remember, my son. Ask properly and thank properly. Conduct yourself this way with your wife, with other people and above all with the Almighty, and you will always have a beautiful, happy life.

— 7 —

The Seeds of Hatred

My dear son,

I want to talk to you about the subject of hatred.

Hatred! In my mind's eye, I can see you recoil even as you read these words. What has hatred to do with you and your wife, such a beautiful, happily married couple? Your home is full of love. Why should I talk to you about hatred?

I'll tell you why. Because it is important to build your defenses early on. I have a friend who is a surgeon. He tells me that in medical school they used to have the students scrub for twenty or thirty minutes to disinfect their hands before they were allowed into surgery.

"Twenty minutes!" I exclaimed. "Why, no matter how dirty my hands get, if I wash them for two or three minutes they are squeaky clean. Why should you have to scrub for twenty minutes or more?"

"Because what you call squeaky clean is not good enough. When a patient is in surgery, he is so vulnerable to infection that we have to make sure there is not a single germ on our hands. These germs burrow into the cracks and crevices, and it is not so easy to dislodge them. When you think your hands are squeaky clean, you can be sure that if you looked at them under the microscope you would see hordes of germs on parade. So we scrub and scrub and scrub some more, and hopefully, we get them all."

It is the same with hatred. Tiny little germs of hatred can lodge in the cracks and crevices of your relationship without your even knowing it and, if you don't want them to grow and flourish, you have to scrub them out from the beginning.

I imagine you are still puzzled by what I am saying. I don't blame you. The idea of hatred in your marriage is so alien to you. I understand. But let me define hatred to you and, then perhaps, it will become a little clearer.

I once picked up a friend of mine at the airport in the middle of the winter. Do you want to take a guess at the country from which he was arriving? Did you say Argentina? Exactly right. How did you guess?

My friend collected his luggage, and we were ready to go.

"Where is your coat?" I asked him. "It's cold outside."

"My coat is in my luggage," he said. "It's a bother to take it out."

"Trust me," I said. "Take it out and put it on. I've just been outside, and it's cold out there."

"Nah. It's not necessary. We're not going very far, just from the terminal to the car. Believe me, I don't need a coat."

It was no use trying to persuade him, so we went out like that, I in my coat with a woolen scarf around my neck and he in a lightweight jacket. As soon as we stepped out, we were hit by a blast of arctic air.

"B-r-r-r," he shouted. "It's freezing here."

"Well, I don't want to say that I told you so, but I told you that it was cold outside."

"Cold?" he said. "This you call cold? This is the North Pole!"

You see what happened here? He comes from Argentina, which has a climate like that of California, warm and mild all the time. When they say "cold" in Argentina they mean that the temperature is in the sixties or fifties degrees Fahrenheit. So, when I told him that it was cold, he was convinced that he would be fine. It is not that far from the terminal to the car. Had I told him that the temperature was down in the teens, with a wind-chill factor south of zero, he would have gotten the message clearly.

So, when I want to talk about hatred, you have to understand what I mean by the word hatred. After all, with a heart full of love, how can you even think about such a subject? But hatred is as natural to the human heart as love; it can sprout in any heart. You have to learn how to recognize it and how to root it out, so that it is completely banished from your heart.

When I was a child in you-know-where, my father used to tell me stories about the little towns and villages in his native Germany. In his village, there were so few people that it used to be difficult to bring together a *minyan*. They used to appoint a certain boy to go from house to house and call the people to the *minyan*. One day, an older villager suffered a massive heart attack. While the doctors worked on him, they sent the boy around to muster the villagers for reciting some emergency *Tehillim*. The village was close-knit, and in every home the people were as shocked to hear the news as if a tragedy had occurred in their own immediate family. They grabbed their hats and ran to the *shul* to join in saying *Tehillim*.

One of the villagers, however, broke the mold. The boy knocked on his door, and he flung it open with a broad smile on his face. He looked at the boy and laughed and danced around the room.

"Come, would you like to join me for a dance?" he said to the boy.

"Not now," said the boy. "A terrible thing has happened."

"You mean that so-and-so had a heart attack?"

"Yes," said the boy. "They're saying *Tehillim*. Will you come?"

"Come to say *Tehillim*? Are you joking? I am jumping for joy that he had a heart attack. I couldn't be happier. That man is my oldest enemy, and this is my moment of greatest joy!"

Such hatred! Can you imagine? The Dubno Maggid writes that extreme hatred can suppress the compassion that is inborn in every Jew. I must admit that I personally have not witnessed such intense hatred, but I have seen some fairly awful examples.

A couple once came to me to seek advice about their child who was being very difficult at home and in school. After speaking to them for a while, it appeared to me that this very complicated child was the product of the parents' discord which was played out all too often in the presence of the child.

After asking the child to wait in another room, I demonstrated to the parents how their daily displays of antagonism and constant fighting were directly related to their child's problems. I saw on their faces that my words had penetrated to their hearts, and I proposed a plan to rebuild a calm and loving atmosphere in the home. They both agreed.

"Wonderful," I said. "Now, in order for this plan to work, each of you must take the initiative and change your attitude immediately."

The husband sprang up from his seat. "What! After all that I have to take from her, I should all of a sudden talk to her like to a normal person? I never heard such a ridiculous thing in my life. If she decides to change and act differently toward me for a while, I will consider making changes as well. But I should start? Get real!"

Now it was her turn to jump up from her seat. "Oh, and I suppose he expects me to make changes, while he just sits back and judges me. Like he always does. It's enough that I'm not demanding that he beg my forgiveness, but the first move has definitely got to be his. The idea!"

This went on back and forth, and I could not get them to agree. I begged them to lay their grudges aside for the sake of the child. It did not do me any good. Their hatred for each other burned so strongly that it suppressed their natural feelings for their child.

Hatred among human beings, says the Dubno Maggid, is similar to hatred among the wild beasts. An animal wants to tear apart and destroy its foe. Its hatred is instinctive and uncontrollable. A human being, however, can control his emotions, but when his hatred breaks loose, it is as vicious and destructive as the hatred of an animal.

How can such a thing happen between husband and wife? How can two people who once nurtured a love for each other in their hearts turn around so completely that they now hate each other?

These are really very perplexing questions, but the Dubno Maggid sheds some light on the matter. It begins, he explains, when a person sees his friend acting in a degrading way or doing something wrong. He cannot get it out of his mind and, subconsciously, he begins to harbor a little antipathy against his friend. He dwells on it continuously, and that small seed swells into a monstrous hatred. These overlays of hatred can be so powerful that the closest friend can become abominable in his eyes.

I'll show you how such a thing happened on a large scale long ago in Jewish history. During the times of Yirmiyahu, the Egyptians made an alliance with the Kingdom of Yehudah, and they sent an army to support the Jewish forces. Along the way they came to the Sea of Reeds, which reminded them that their ancestors had drowned when the Jewish people had come forth from Egypt almost a thousand years earlier, and a hatred against the Jews was awakened in their hearts. This hatred festered in them until they began to have visions — delusions — of large objects floating in the sea. Their hatred continued to boil until those floating objects appeared to them as bloated dead bodies. Their hatred turned to fury and, in anger, they returned to Egypt and refused to come to the aid of the Jewish forces.

Here was a totally illogical delusion. Is it possible for the bodies of drowned Egyptians to float to the surface after almost a thousand years? Ridiculous. Such thoughts are a sign of an unhinged mind. And yet, this was the connection the Egyptians made in their hate-stoked minds. The Egyptians lost their mental balance, to a certain extent, by the reawakening of the old hatred in their hearts.

Hatred distorts reality. It starts reasonably enough with the Sea of Reeds as a reminder of the ignominious defeat of the ancient Egyptians, but then it loses touch with reality and, soon, hundreds of thousands of people can see phantom bodies floating in the sea.

Something of the sort can also happen between husband and wife or, for that matter, in any personal relationships. A small misstep arouses resentment and, before you know it, everything is blown way out of proportion. Reality is distorted to the point that it becomes unrecognizable.

I see this often in my involvement with marital problems. When I hear the first side of the story, I am presented with a picture of a real ogre. I shudder to meet this person. However, when the spouse comes in, I usually see no sign of the monster that was just described to me. Instead, I see a kind, soft-spoken human being. How could such a thing be? Obviously, the anger of the spouse distorted his or her sense of reality until the other spouse took on the image of a monster from fantasyland.

My child, the seeds of this kind of hatred are really common-place in everyone's life. They are the little irritations and annoyances that inevitably arise when two people live together or are otherwise closely associated day in and day out.

How then are you supposed to react when you are face to face with irritations? One way to respond is with anger, which expresses itself, in this case, as a form of hatred, which leads directly to quarrels, as it written in *Mishlei* (10:12), "Hatred arouses strife." The disintegration of the relationship has begun. The hatred and the quarreling distort the image of the spouse, highlighting the negative and obscuring the positive. This leads to more hatred and more quarreling and more distortion, one following the other in an endless vicious cycle until only the spouse's negative side remains visible. The positive side completely disappears from view.

All too many times have I heard troubled people speak of the beautiful early years of their marriages and then suggest that their spouses need psychiatric treatment. Why do they suppose their spouses have changed so drastically? What has transformed their loving spouses into mental patients? Why don't their spouses' other associates see this decline in their mental health? It all stems from a distorted view brought on by small irritations that set off an uncontrolled chain reaction.

There is also another way to deal with small irritations. The end of the verse states (ibid.), "But love covers all sins." It is far better to respond to an irritation with love, because this will keep things in perspective. It will help you realize that the irritation is such a minor thing in comparison with the great blessing in your life that is your wife. The coating of love will cause her to continue to shine in your eyes even when she has caused you some small irritation, and your feelings for her will not be damaged.

A mother buys her little daughter a beautiful new dress for a family wedding. Just as the family is about to leave for the hall, the little girl appears with chocolate ice cream stains on her dress. How does the mother react? She is obviously upset and irritated, but does her loving relationship with her child suffer? Of course not. She cleans her up, utters a few scolding words and deals with the situation. Then she hugs and kisses her child, and they go off happily to the wedding. Later, she even laughs about it when she tells her friends what happened. Her love for her child covers the child's little faults.

Avoid problems, my son. When a minor irritation appears, brush it away. Don't let the dust build up until it becomes a problem. Give a coating of love to each little irritation that arises, and it will disappear right before your eyes. Think about how wonderful your wife is. Think about what a blessing she is to you in every aspect of your life. And then consider the small irritation, and you will see that it is really insignificant. Compared to what you have, it is nothing.

⁓

My dear son,

You know that the heart is a complex thing. There are so many emotions that course through the heart, and sometimes you experience a few of them at the same time. However, writes the Chazon Ish in *Emunah U'Bitachon*, love and hatred never appear in the heart at the same time. A heart that is feeling love cannot feel hatred. A heart that hates cannot love.

Let me tell you a story about my friend, the talented *rebbe* I mentioned a few letters ago. One year, he had a very contentious class; the boys fought all the time. Try as he might, he could not get them to stop.

Then he had an idea. He brought a walkie-talkie to class and bided his time. He did not have to wait too long. Two minutes into recess, David and Eli were fighting about some trivial matter. "I hate you," David screamed at Eli, at the top of his lungs.

"Okay, stop right now," said the *rebbe*. "We're going to take care of this once and for all, in a mature way. We're going to have a trial in front of the class. Each of you, David and Eli, will have the opportunity to present your sides of the story, then the class will vote to decide who is right."

The idea of a debate with the class voting to decide the winner captured everyone's imagination. David and Eli were the most excited of all. David could hardly sit still. "So when do we begin, *rebbe*?" he asked.

"Right now," said the *rebbe*. "Here, you see this walkie-talkie? You take one of the units and go out into the hall. Prepare you case, and when I give you the signal, present your case to the class over the walkie-talkie. After you finish, it will be Eli's turn."

David grabbed the walkie-talkie unit and ran out into the hall. A few minutes later, the *rebbe* pressed the Talk button on the walkie-talkie. "Are you ready?" he asked.

"Yes, I am," David replied

The *rebbe* pressed the Talk button again and said, "Then go ahead. Begin!" But this time, the *rebbe* held the Talk button down even after he finished speaking.

Two minutes later, a frustrated David came running back in to class. "It's not fair!" he shouted. "Someone was holding the Talk button down, and no one could hear anything I said."

"Exactly!" said the *rebbe*. "You've just made an important discovery. When you push the Talk button you stop incoming messages. You and Eli have been such good friends for such a long time. Whenever you look at each other, you should be feeling love and friendship. But when you push that angry Hatred button, you stop all feelings of love from flowing into your hearts."

This is what I have observed with many married couples experiencing marital problems. They get angry with each other, the flow of resentment stems the flow of loving feelings and, suddenly, they think they are incompatible. Sometimes I wish I could put them in the hall with a walkie-talkie, but you cannot do this with grown-ups. You have to talk to them and convince them that the deep feelings of mutual love are still there, buried underneath an avalanche of resentment and hurt.

If so, how do we stem the flow of negative feelings when we get angry and upset? How can we prevent the impulsive resentment from snowballing into the perception of incompatibility?

The Torah gives us the best model for preventive measures. Listen to the way it is presented, more or less, in Midrash Tanchuma. Two enemies are traveling on the road in the same direction. They do not speak to each other, and they keep a safe distance apart. Each one is leading a heavily laden donkey.

Suddenly, one man's donkey collapses under the weight of its load. The other man sees his enemy's misfortune, and he recalls that there is a *mitzvah* in the Torah (*Shemos* 23:5) to help one's enemy in just such circumstances. So he stops to help him in icy silence. Without talking to his enemy, he helps him reload the donkey, and they continue on their way.

The man stays close to his enemy's donkey, because in its weakened condition, it may fall again. He speaks the barest minimum to his enemy, just that which is necessary to keep the load from collapsing again. However, as they continue, the ice thaws somewhat, and the conversation flows more smoothly. Both of these enemies taste the sweet flavor of peace. They see each other in a new light, and they stop at an inn to break bread together. They eat and drink in harmony, and the two enemies become friends.

Look, my son, and marvel at the wisdom of the Torah. How does the Torah bring these two enemies together? How does the Torah stop the flow of hatred that is obscuring all other feelings? By obligating the man to help his enemy on the most basic human level. His enemy is in trouble. Help him. This simple act builds a bridge between these two hostile hearts, and this bridge breaks through the wall of silence, interrupting the flow of hatred and allowing other feelings to rise to the surface.

When a husband is angry with his wife and the flow of hatred prevents him from relating to her on the deep emotional level, he should never withdraw into a funk and ignore her. Despite his anger, he should continue to help her in anything she needs. This is the best preventive for avoiding marital problems. Helping her on the most basic human level will stop the flow of hatred, and the feelings of love will rise to the surface in all their power and beauty.

When my father went away on business trips, my mother used to say that she was left behind as a *strohwitwe*, a straw widow. How sensitive are the feelings of a woman! Her husband was temporarily absent, and she already felt she was missing part of herself. She already felt as if she was experiencing a form of widowhood.

I think that when a husband gets angry and gives his wife the silent treatment, he is causing a similar commotion in her heart. He may think he needs a little time to mind his own business and cool off, and perhaps send a message to his wife of his extreme annoyance, but he does not understand what he is causing in her heart. I believe he is causing her to feel like a straw divorcee, if there is such an expression. It is truly a tragedy, because this is not what either of them wants. However, if he continues to help her and speak to her — despite his annoyance — the flow of anger and resentment will subside, and the flow of love will return in full force.

— 8 —

Outbursts of Anger

My dear son,

They say that the Chazon Ish once picked up a flower and spent such a long time intensely examining it that he actually became exhausted. Now, if you or I were to pick up a flower to look at it, I don't think we would exhaust ourselves. What is the difference?

You see, most people relate to their experiences on an emotional level. They see a beautiful flower. They pick it up to take a close look and see even more beauty, and then they are finished. What else is there to see? So, they take a final whiff and go on to something else.

The Chazon Ish, however, was fascinated by the Divine wisdom that went into the creation of that flower. What made the flower work? Exactly how did the parts fit together and what gave them such a beautiful appearance? It took him a long time to conduct his in-depth examination, so long that it eventually exhausted him.

You find this difference in approach in many situations in life, especially with regard to pain. Something causes us pain — how do we react? We immediately label it as negative and hostile, and we recoil in anger and frustration. But that is not necessarily the best approach. Pain is not necessarily such a bad thing.

Look at it this way: A paralyzed person feels no sensation in his arms or legs. So look at the bright side, right? At least he feels no pain if something should strike him, right? Wrong. A person who feels pain will be forewarned to protect himself from danger, while a person who feels no pain might suffer severe damage without even being aware of it.

If so, how should you respond to pain? You can respond emotionally, getting angry and frustrated, or you can respond with wisdom, bearing the discomfort while you investigate and discover its causes. You can use pain to your advantage. It should be a welcome warning sign.

You know, the worst tumors are those that cause no pain. They grow and grow, spreading their malignant poison through the body before anyone is aware of their existence. By the time they are discovered, it is often much too late to do anything about it. A tumor that is painful at the outset, however, can often be treated before it becomes too powerful. Early detection is the key to health, and pain is its messenger.

The same applies to a marriage. If you can address resentments and ill feelings when they are born, there is an excellent chance that they can be dispelled and perfect harmony can be recaptured. On the other hand, if they are allowed to fester and grow, they can take on a life of their own. Later, when their existence is discovered, it may be exceedingly difficult to eradicate them and repair the damage.

So you see, my son, how fortunate we are that the Creator instilled in the nature of the woman the propensity to react with outbursts of anger when her hurt rises above the level of tolerance. The intelligent husband responds to these outbursts with wisdom, rather than emotion. He does not get angry and frustrated. He does not lash out in retaliation and make matters even worse. No, he takes note of her pain and hurt, he investigates, he discovers the problems and he corrects them.

The Gemara tells us (*Berachos* 51b) that Ulla joined Rav Nachman for a meal. Ulla said *Bircas HaMazon* over a cup of wine, and afterwards, he gave Rav Nachman some wine from the *kos shel berachah*. Rav Nachman's wife Yalta was in a different room at the time, and Rav Nachman suggested to Ulla that he send her some wine, as well. Ulla declined to do so. When Yalta found out that she had been denied the *kos shel berachah*, she stood up in a fury, stormed into the wine cellar and smashed four hundred casks of wine. The commentators explain that she was impressing upon them the message that the wine from the *kos shel berachah* was as precious to her as four hundred casks of wine.

The word the Gemara uses here for fury is *zihara*, a rather unusual expression of anger that is mentioned only in connection with women. When speaking of the anger of men, the Gemara will speak of *rogez*, *ris'cha* or something similar — but women react with *zihara*. What is *zihara*?

We get a clue from the Gemara (*Yoma* 28b) which tells us that the *zihara* of sunlight is more intense than ordinary sunlight. When there is a break in the cloud cover in the sky, the sunlight that bursts through is more intense than sunlight on a cloudless day.

A woman's anger is like the *zihara*. It is ordinarily contained and restricted but, when she is deeply hurt, it bursts through the restrictions. That is why it is particularly intense. The wise husband does not react to the anger itself, which is only a symptom, but to its root cause. He seeks to discover the underlying cause of the anger. Then he does his best to remove it and restore serenity and peace of mind to his devoted wife.

A young man once approached me after Maariv on a Friday night in the winter. He was all upset about a situation that had arisen at home earlier that day.

"I don't know what to do," he said. "How can I go home after what happened today?"

"Perhaps it would help," I said, "if you told me a little about it."

"Well, you see, my wife is very organized and orderly. Every Friday, she does all the cooking and cleaning for Shabbos and makes sure everything is just right. So, today, because it's such a short day in the winter, I was running around from store to store. Then I schlepped all the packages home. My wife had just mopped the floor, and I walked in with my snowy boots and got the floor a little dirty. She just exploded at me and gave me a tongue lashing, so how am I supposed to go home now? Am I supposed to just smile at her and say, 'Good Shabbos' as if nothing happened?"

"Look," I said. "Let's approach this calmly. Instead of being overcome with emotion, let's see if we can do this with a little wisdom. First let's learn through a piece of Gemara about Yalsa, the wife of Rav Nachman. All right?"

The young man nodded. So we learned the Gemara, and I explained to him about *zihara*.

"Now," I said, "let's try to figure out why she yelled at you. Do you think she hates you?"

"Of course not," he said. "She does everything for me."

"Then why was she upset? Does she care so much about her floor?"

"No."

"Then what was it?"

"I suppose it's because she wanted everything perfect for Shabbos."

"Exactly! So we know that she is a very special person that cares deeply about honoring Shabbos properly. We also know that when she feels a deep hurt, she can react with an outburst of anger called a *zihara*. To your wife's credit, what upsets her is a deficiency in honoring Shabbos. You should respect her for this, and find it in your heart to forgive her for lashing out at you. She did not mean to hurt you. Do you think you can do this?"

The young man took a deep breath and gave me a sheepish smile. Then he wished me a "Good Shabbos" and went home.

Yes, my dear son, it is a hard thing that I had asked this young man to do, but I think it was the right thing. It could only bring benefit to him and to his wife.

$$\backsim$$

My dear son,

Last time, I told you about how a woman can sometimes have an outburst of anger, and I told you a story about a young man who tracked snow on his wife's freshly mopped floor.

If this ever happens to you, you have to keep your wits about you. I know it can be very painful to bear the brunt of such an outburst, but always let your wisdom be your guide, not your emotions.

Let me tell you a story about another young man who once approached me with a similar problem. This young man's wife had really lashed out at him and said such nasty things that it seemed as if she had lost her feelings for him.

The young man wisely remained silent and did not get into a shouting match with his wife. He was very upset and thought through the situation again and again, but he could not find where he had been at fault. So after his wife had calmed down, he presented her with his side of the story and complained about some of the things she had said, as if she did not care about him any more.

His wife was shocked. She agreed that he had really been blameless, but she had no recollection of saying all those awful things. On the contrary, she was upset that he would entertain the thought that she had lost her feelings for him.

The young man came to discuss the matter with me. He agreed readily that his wife was sincere and that she apparently did not remember saying any of those things, but he was concerned that she might not be quite 100% stable.

I showed him the Gemara in *Yevamos* (116a) that discusses the rule that a woman who had discord with her husband is not believed if she says that he died. The Gemara wants to know what is considered discord. Rav Yehudah says, "If the woman told her husband, 'I want a divorce!'" The Gemara argues that this is not really proof of marital discord, since "all women say this." *Rashi* explains that they are liable to say such things when they get angry, but that does not prove that there is discord in the relationship.

Apparently, it is the nature of women to say such things when they get angry, even though there is nothing wrong with the relationship. These words do not mirror her true emotions.

"So you see," I said to the young man, "she may have used words that were far removed from her real feelings, so far that they did not even register in her mind. They just came out by themselves, as a reflex. That's why she does not remember them."

What can so upset a woman that she reacts with an outburst of harsh words that she does not even remember afterwards? Very often, it is guilt. She wants so much to be the perfect mother and homemaker that she sometimes does not live up to her own expectations and feels guilty. When she is feeling distraught and inadequate, she may lash out at you, even though you have done nothing wrong.

You don't think this can happen? Then let me remind you about something that happened with you a number of years ago, when you were a child, but not such a little one.

I am sure you remember how you always excelled in your studies and how proud you were to bring home good marks on your report cards. It is good to want to excel, and we were equally proud of your accomplishments. Well, one day, I came home and saw the envelope from the report card lying on the table. Eager to see your grades, I asked you for the report card.

Do you remember how you reacted? I'm sure you do, since it was completely out of character. You screamed and yelled at me and were altogether disrespectful — then you ran off to your room.

Instead of being insulted and offended, I immediately suspected that your grades were not as high as they usually were. My suspicions were confirmed when your mother showed me the report card. I then responded as a father concerned for the welfare of his child should react. I understood that your feelings of guilt and inadequacy had sparked this uncharacteristic outburst, and my first priority was to help you rebuild your self-esteem and help you succeed in school.

You have to respond in a similar way in your own home when you are faced with a seemingly irrational and disproportionate outburst of anger. Be calm and use your wisdom and intelligence. Sniff out the situation, find out what is bothering her and see if you can help. But rest assured that she loves you and appreciates you as much as ever.

I am not telling you not to be upset when you hear such words, but to listen to them in the context of the situation. The Gemara says that a woman in labor cries out that she never wants to have children again — but does she mean it? Soon after the pain subsides, she is once again as eager as ever to have more children. That was her pain talking, not her. You have to understand that sometimes when she lashes out at you it is her pain or guilt talking, and her words are not a true barometer of her feelings toward you.

My dear son,

As you grow older, you will discover that different people react differently to different situations. Sometimes people react by withdrawing or running away. This is not necessarily a sign of cowardice. It may simply be an instinctive reaction to a stressful situation.

There was once a bombing in an office building in Buenos Aires, and one of the men who escaped from the building was in such shock that he did not stop running for three days. Did he think that his running would make him or his family safer? Of course not, but he ran nonetheless, because he could not deal with the stress.

I once read a story about an attempted revolt in the concentration camps. A group of prisoners had smuggled in arms and buried them in the ground. They were waiting for an opportune moment to distribute the weapons, and the prisoners would rise up against their oppressors. One night, they heard that the Germans were planning to liquidate their block the next day, sending them all to the gas chambers. Clearly, there was no more time to wait, and the revolt was scheduled for the following morning.

When morning came, however, the leader of the revolt was nowhere in sight. He had committed suicide during the night. Now why did this brave man, who had planned and coordinated the imminent revolt, kill himself? Was he afraid that he might be killed? Not likely, since he knew he was headed for the gas chamber anyway. Besides, he could have just refused to participate in the revolt. No, it was a reaction to the unbearable stress of the situation. When it became too much for him, he simply "ran away" and committed suicide.

Rabbeinu Yonah writes (*Mishlei* 19:26) that women do not have the same capacity to endure stress as do men. The nature of a woman is to "run away" when a situation becomes too emotionally charged. It does not mean that she is not a brave and courageous person. It simply means that a tidal wave of emotion can cause her to seek escape, because such is the nature of women.

An outburst of anger is a form of escape. When your wife feels that the emotions in a situation are too overwhelming, she may seek to escape the situation by making angry comments that bring the situation to an end. Remember, this is an instinctive reaction, not a conscious choice.

When the Rambam enumerates (*Hil. Ishus* 16:19) the obligations of the husband to his wife, he includes the instruction "not to be a *ragzan*, an angry person." When he enumerates the obligations of the wife, however, he does not mention that she should not be an angry person, only that she should respect her husband and hold him in high esteem.

Why is this so?

Certainly, a woman is required to control her anger with her husband, just as she must control her anger with all people, but the special outbursts of anger that might be sparked by the intense emotionality of the relationship are sometimes so instinctive and reflexive that they are simply beyond her control. The husband, however, is by nature better able to control his emotions, and therefore he bears a greater responsibility to promote peace and harmony in the home. He should not react to her angry outbursts with anger of his own. Rather, he should give her reassurance and emotional support and thereby relieve the tension of the situation.

My dear son, there have been times in your life that you have taken a greater share of the burden on your own shoulders. Work had to be done, things had to be accomplished, and you did not wait around for others to do their part. You just took it upon yourself to do what needed to be done. You should take the same approach in your marriage.

You may find that the burden of maintaining a harmonious atmosphere in your home is falling on your shoulders more than on your wife's shoulders, but that is all right. You are the one who is better equipped to deflect anger and bring peace and harmony to your home. The responsibility is yours. Do what needs to be done. It is well worth it.

⌒

My dear son,

It would not surprise me if you feel a little overwhelmed by the prospect of conducting a successful relationship with a woman who loves you but whom you really don't understand all that well. I want you to know that the Almighty has given you the tools not only to cope, but to be successful. He has given you *sechel*, intelligence. The important thing is not to get lazy and react on instinct. If you approach all situations with that wonderful innate intelligence that the Almighty has implanted in you, the atmosphere of your home will be full of love, harmony and joy.

You know, when I first came to the United States, I was eager to learn English. I listened to the conversations of my friends in order to learn new words and add them to my vocabulary. There was one word, however, that thoroughly confused me. It was a very long word, and my friends used it all the time. They would refer to things as a "whatchamacallit."

What is a whatchamacallit? Try as I did, I could not figure out the meaning of this word. I finally realized that it really has no meaning. It is a word that people use when they do not want to invest in the effort to find the appropriate word for what they are trying to say. They cannot be bothered to engage that wonderful gift — their intelligence — to find the right expression. So instead, they just say "whatchamacallit" and expect the other person, if he so chooses, to figure it out for himself.

Well, that kind of attitude will not get you far in life and certainly not in your marriage. You have to keep your intelligence sharpened and in use, at all times.

Before the war, the *rav* of the city of Mir, Poland, was Rav Elya Baruch Kamai. A woman once came to ask him a *she'eilah* and found him learning Gemara. She looked a little more closely and noticed that it was *Mesechta Bava Kamma*.

"*Bava Kamma*?" she exclaimed. "Why, my young son just finished learning *Bava Kamma*. He was tested, and he knows it perfectly. How can it be that you are still learning *Bava Kamma*?"

The *rav* smiled and told her, "There are two *Bava Kammas*."

A clever answer, don't you think? Because it is true. The *Bava Kamma* a young boy learns in *mesivta* bears almost no resemblance to the *Bava Kamma* that a *talmid chacham* learns.

The same applies to a married man's understanding of the feminine mind. Before you were married, your exposure to feminine thinking had been through your mother, sisters, relatives and others. In all these instances, it was like learning *Bava Kamma* in *mesivta*. Now that you are married, you must approach the understanding of women like a new *mesechta*, because you must learn it on an entirely different level.

The Torah tells us (*Bereishis* 2:18) that the Almighty created Chavah for Adam as an *eizer kenegdo*, a helpmate against him. The Rishonim explain that Chavah was the exact opposite of Adam and, therefore, she was the perfect match for him. A man does not see the feminine side, and how it is his exact opposite, until he marries and begins his relationship with his wife.

At first, when a man sees the full manifestations of his wife's feminine personality, he is naturally inclined to measure it against his own, and he may reach the erroneous conclusion that that there is something wrong. That is when it is critical that he uses his intelligence. He has to understand that his wife is the most wonderful person, and that the Almighty, in His infinite wisdom, decided to create man and woman with opposite natures, so that they should complement each other perfectly.

The Gemara (*Shabbos* 62a) very wisely characterizes women as a nation unto themselves. This gives us an excellent insight into understanding women. You have to understand that getting married is like traveling to a foreign country and, if you want to be successful, you need to learn the unfamiliar language and customs. This is not an easy thing.

During the last years of my parents' lives, I visited them in Buenos Aires three times a year. Now, I grew up there, and I should be familiar with the place — and I was visiting three times a year. Nevertheless, each time I came, I went through a period of adjustment to attune myself with the Hispanic way of speaking and thinking before I could feel perfectly at home. You can imagine how hard it is for someone coming to a country that he really does not know.

So you see, my dear son, you have your work cut out for you. You have to keep your intelligence engaged at all times and learn the language, nature, feelings, expressions, sensitivities and customs of this "nation of women" to which your wonderful wife belongs.

Let me finish with two quick anecdotes. I was once an emergency substitute for a class of young children learning the *aleph-beis*. I taught them the next scheduled letter and, by the end of the day, they all knew it. I felt very proud and accomplished. The next day, to my dismay, they had all forgotten everything I had taught them. You can imagine how disappointed I was.

When I told the regular teacher about my experience, he smiled and said, "You made a basic mistake. You assumed that young children absorb knowledge just as you do, but they do not. In order to teach children of this age successfully, you have to understand how their minds work."

I would say, then, that in order to communicate successfully with your wife you have to understand how her mind works it works differently than yours does. Don't you agree?

One more little story. A friend of mine in Israel arranged a meeting between a girl from Argentina and a boy from Italy. There was no problem with a language barrier, since they both spoke Hebrew fluently. Nonetheless, the *shidduch* almost did not get off the ground. You see, the first time they met, the boy said to her, "*Ciao*," pronounced "chow." This is a casual way of saying hello in Italian. He didn't know, however, that in the colloquial Spanish spoken in Argentina, the homonymic word *chau* means good-bye. So, according to the girl's understanding, here was a boy that was greeting her by saying "good-bye." Very strange.

Mixed signals obviously create problems, and the same is true for your marriage. In order to have a happy marriage, you have to learn the true meaning of your wife's words, actions and reactions. And in order to do this, you must use your intelligence all the time. It will require some effort on your part, but believe me, it is well worth it.

— *9* —

*Wise
Apologies*

My dear son,

I want to tell about an experience I once had in the yeshivah. A boy came to me during the month of Elul and told me that his *chavrusa* had made a very offensive comment to him. The boy was so deeply hurt that he was unable to concentrate on the Gemara for weeks.

A short while later, I said a *shmuess* in the yeshivah about the importance of asking forgiveness before Yom Kippur. As I was walking out of the *beis midrash,* I overheard this boy's *chavrusa* say to him, "Please forgive me."

I didn't say anything, but inwardly I cringed. Did this young fellow think that he would get away with the terrible thing he did, by simply mouthing a few words?

I was reminded of a story that happened with a friend of your mother's from Montevideo, Uruguay, whom I will refer to as Shoshanah, for the sake of privacy. Shoshanah's little daughter had been diagnosed as having a hole in her heart. There was only one doctor in the world who did the complicated procedure that the little girl needed, and he was in Boston. So Shoshanah traveled all the way to Boston and, since your mother was in her ninth month at the time, I went in her stead to Boston to help with the communication between Shoshanah and the Boston medical people.

Shoshanah met with the surgeon and the cardiologist together. The surgeon went to a large blackboard in the back of the room and drew a rough sketch of a heart. Then he added the holes in the appropriate places. "You see," he said. "We go right in here, and we just sew it all up."

The cardiologist saw the look of relief on Shoshanah's face and exclaimed, "It's not so simple, madam!" He did not want to give her false hope about the operation, which was extremely complicated. He wanted her to face the reality. The surgeon had made it all seem like child's play, so the cardiologist felt obligated to warn her that "it's not so simple." *Baruch Hashem*, the operation was successful, but the scene stayed in my mind for a long time.

"It's not so simple!" I wanted to yell at the insensitive *chavrusa*. "You think you can insult a boy so badly that he cannot concentrate for weeks, and then just wipe it all away by saying, 'Please forgive me'? Do you think that wipes away the hurt and humiliation? Do you think those few words that roll so effortlessly off your tongue have healed the scars of the wound you inflicted?"

The Midrash compares the emotions of the human heart to a well so deep that, in order to draw water, many ropes have to be tied together securely and a pail attached at the end. You cannot simply bend over and scoop out some water with a pail held in your hand. The water is too far away.

The depths of the human heart also cannot be reached so easily. You have to tie together many ropes. You have to talk, appease, comfort and pacify with wisdom and intelligence, and keep doing it until the pain has been relieved. According to the *Rishonim*, one can determine half a person's wisdom by watching how he appeases other people. It takes very little wisdom to ask forgiveness in a casual, cavalier fashion, but it also accomplishes very little. Asking forgiveness is not enough. The Gemara repeatedly tells us that you have to be *mefayes*, to appease, the injured person, even if the assault was only verbal. *Piyus* takes wisdom. It takes time and insight and sensitivity.

Let me give you an example just to make my point perfectly clear. Imagine there was a man named Moshe from a modern community who is quite a popular speaker in his circles. He is invited to a *bar-mitzvah* in his family, which include members who are more *yeshivish*. He is asked to speak, and he goes on for so long that people are frustrated. A few of them make derogatory remarks, and he is offended.

What do they have to do to be *mefayes* him? It depends.

If they did not demean his speaking ability — just the length of his speech — then his ego probably was not bruised. All they would have to say is that his speech was wonderful but that he probably lost track of the time in his enthusiasm for his subject. They certainly did not mean to hurt him, and this type of response would probably be just fine.

However, what if they had said that he might be a good speaker for modern audiences, but that he totally bored a more *heimishe* crowd? In this case, it would be insufficient to say that they did not mean to hurt him. It would be like trying to draw water from a deep well with a handheld pail. After destroying his self-image as a good speaker, they would have to strain their wisdom and intelligence to find some way to touch his heart and repair the damage. A simple "I'm sorry" would not do.

Now, the wise apology does not necessarily have to be longer and more elaborate. It just needs to address the hurt in the right way.

Let me tell you a story. A certain boy had arranged to meet a girl for a *shidduch*. Before he actually met her, however, he discovered that there were some problems with the family. Not knowing what to do, he called a prominent *rav* for advice. The *rav* advised him to go meet the girl and be polite and then decline to pursue the *shidduch* further. Somehow the girl found out afterwards what the *rav* had advised the boy to do, and she was deeply hurt and offended.

Years passed. The boy married someone else. The girl also married and was very happy with her new husband. A few months after she got married, she wrote a letter to the *rav* in which she described all the pain and suffering she had endured because of the advice he had given that boy. The *rav* found the letter disturbing. He knew that she was now happily married, and he wondered why she would write such a letter so many years after the incident had taken place. Why had her suffering surfaced anew, now that she was enjoying such a beautiful married life?

After careful consideration, the *rav* wrote her a brief letter in which he apologized for having caused her pain and suffering, but he did not address any of the issues involved. He also congratulated her on her recent marriage and sent her a modest check as a wedding gift.

Shortly afterward, the *rav* received a second letter from the young woman, in which she thanked him for the wedding gift. She went on to say that she now realized that the *rav* had acted correctly and properly and that she would frame the check and keep it as a memento of the greatness of some of the *rabbanim* of our generation.

What do you say about this story, my son? A real mystery, isn't it? Here the young woman writes a long letter to the *rav*, pages and pages filled with grievances and hurt, and what does he do? He responds with a brief apology and a check! Mysterious. But wait, the mystery deepens. How does the young woman respond to the *rav's* apology? She accepts it wholeheartedly and even goes on to praise the *rav* for how he has handled her. And what about all those grievances that the *rav* did not even bother to address? Why was she so happy, even though the *rav* had not addressed a single one of them?

The answer, my dear son, is in the topic we have been discussing. The human heart is a deep well, full of complicated emotions. If you manage to touch the right emotions with the right words, you can work wonders.

Think for a minute. Why was this young woman suffering so much pain when she wrote her letter to the *rav*? If she had written such a letter before she was married, we would understand it better. She would be worried that she would not be able to get married because of her family problems. But that was all in the past. She had married well, and she was happy. So why was she still feeling all the hurt reflected in her letter?

The answer seems quite clear. Before she was married, she was unsure of herself, because of her family situation. When the *rav* gave his advice, therefore, it was a shattering blow to her self-esteem. Even though she was bright, personable and talented, she felt worthless. True, she did get married leaving her troubles behind, but her self-esteem was still shattered. The wounds were still open, and these prompted her to write her letter to the *rav*.

The wise *rav* understood what was in her heart. He knew she did not need explanations and excuses. All she needed was to regain her self-esteem, to reaffirm for herself that she was indeed a worthy person. The *rav's* letter of apology, brief but earnest, gave her back her self-esteem, especially since it was accompanied by a wedding gift, no less! Suddenly, she was transformed from a bitter person to the sunny, confident person who wrote the second letter to the *rav*.

Do you see, my son, how the right words at the appropriate time can be so critically important?

Let me tell you a story. Yes, you guessed it. It is about my youth in Argentina. How did you know?

In our *shul* in Buenos Aires, most of the people were strong supporters of the State of Israel. There was one man, however, a refugee who came to Argentina after the Second World War, who was affiliated with the *Neturei Karta* group and was a staunch opponent of the State. Although he was a respected member of the congregation, his views on the State earned him a great deal of antagonism, especially among the young people.

One day, a group of youngsters mounted a vocal and nasty protest against him in the shul. I was standing nearby, watching, but I was not involved in the protest itself.

A long time later, when I was spending my first Elul in Lakewood, it occurred to me that perhaps I should not have been standing there while this ugly incident was taking place, so I wrote a letter to the man, apologizing for standing there even though I did not participate in the protest.

Five years later, I returned to Argentina to visit my parents for the first time after coming to Lakewood. By that time, this man was already very old and confined to his home. I decided to pay him a visit. Since he did not know I was coming to Buenos Aires, he was surprised to see me but also quite pleased.

We chatted pleasantly for a half hour and then I rose to leave. Suddenly, he pulled out a well-worn paper from the pocket of his robe and said to me, "Do you know what this is?"

It was the letter I had sent him five years earlier! Can you imagine? He must have carried that letter around with him all the time. It was then that I realized the powerful effect of a proper apology.

My dear son,

You asked me to explain to you how you and your former roommate could have such different approaches to your wives. Your roommate used to review and analyze every meeting with her. Did he do this right? Did he do that right? Did he say the right thing in this situation? How about in that situation? He put everything he had done or said under a microscope, never assuming that he had been right. After he got married, however, everything turned around. He was tough with his wife and always so sure of himself. In his own eyes, he could do no wrong.

You, on the other hand, were different. When you were seeing your prospective wife, you were easygoing and relaxed. You did not stop to analyze minutely everything you or she said. You just went on general impressions. After you were married, however, you realized that you had a lot to learn about women and that it was easy to make mistakes.

First of all, I want to tell you that I cannot talk to you about your former roommate specifically, because I do not know him. All I know is what you have told me, and that is not enough to form an opinion.

Did I ever tell you about this young fellow, one of my father's friends back in Germany, whose parents were pressuring him to apply for a certain job? He did not think this profession was for him, but the parental pressure was too strong to ignore. What did he do? He filled out the application in neat, precise German and then he opened his fountain pen and dropped a few ink spots onto the paper. He felt sure that, there in Germany, such a sloppy application would be turned down.

Well, he was wrong. The owner looked at the application and took notice of the intelligence, strict grammar and neatness of the answers. How could it be, he wondered, that such a person would submit a sloppy application without rewriting it? He decided to meet the applicant and see for himself. Once they met, the owner took an immediate liking to him and offered him the job.

So you see, if you speak to me about an aberration in your roommate's behavior, I cannot evaluate it unless I meet with him and talk to him in person for a while.

However, it is certainly true that there are some men who think they are always right. It is rooted in the character trait called *azus*, brazenness. On Yom Kippur, we say again and again to the A-mighty, "We are not so brazen (*azei panim*) as to say, 'We are righteous and have not sinned.'" How can a person carrying a big bundle of sins claim that he is righteous? Only by being brazen, by hardening his heart and his face so that he becomes impervious to all thoughts that he does not want to entertain.

I heard a story about an old non-observant Jew who was approached by a *kiruv* person and invited for a Shabbos. The man shook his head and said, "These things are not for me. I am cut from a different cloth."

He then went on to tell an incredible story. There was a group of young men in his *shtetl* who had wandered from the Torah. They wanted to smoke on Shabbos, so they would go out to the cemetery and smoke in peace.

One Friday night these fellows assembled in the cemetery to smoke, but no one had any matches. Instead of going back for matches, someone hit upon the idea of getting a light from the *ner tamid* on a grave. In order to get to this fire, however, it was necessary to lie down on the grave. One of the young men stretched out on the grave with his cigarette in his mouth — and he died on the spot!

Can you imagine? Right then and there, this young fellow in the best of health, in the prime of his life, is full of youth and vigor one moment and the next moment he is — dead! How frightening that must have been for the rest of the group!

Well, this next part of the story is the most incredible of all. The next Shabbos, the crew got together again in the cemetery to smoke. Business as usual. What about the clear Divine message of the previous week? Nothing. This is brazenness. Strengthen yourself and ignore everything. Be like a stone. Do not reexamine and reassess. Stay the course.

Brazenness, my son, is not limited to corrupt people. Even the best and most wonderful people can fall victim to the lure of brazenness. It is one of the most powerful defense mechanisms in the human psyche, and it shows up in the most unexpected places.

I became close to a young man in the yeshivah — a really wonderful young man. We used to learn together, and his grasp of the Gemara and his insights were simply outstanding. He always sought the truth and rejected anything that appeared to deviate from the truth. In personal relationships, he was pure gold — kind, sensitive and caring.

Well, then came the day when he got his driver's license, a major milestone in the life of most young men. One day he gave a few of us a ride to some event that I cannot recall right now. Among his passengers were a few good, experienced drivers.

What should I tell you? The young man drove terribly. I hung onto the seat and kept closing my eyes, because I really feared for my life. I even resolved to "*bentch*" *Gomel* if I survived the trip. The passengers who were experienced drivers did not just sit silently. They commented gently on his driving, offering helpful suggestions. Believe me, they were very restrained in their comments. If I were in the driver's place, I thought, I would appreciate the good advice.

Then I caught a glance of this young man's face. The soft golden glow was gone, and its place I saw a mask of stone. I could see that he was trying to control his fury at the backseat drivers who had the gall to call his driving anything less than perfect.

What brought about this transformation? Well, it seems obvious that his driving was so important to him that he could not tolerate any criticism of it. He was overcome by brazenness. It did not matter that people were pointing out his flaws in perfectly reasonable and gentle tones. It did not matter that he was always such an advocate of the truth. Right now, he had to turn to stone, to defend his driving. He had to become brazen, because this would allow him to sustain his self-image as a great driver.

In your marriage as well, it is critical that you resist the temptation to become brazen. Train yourself to acknowledge your small faults and missteps and apologize for them. Learn from Yom Kippur. Your apologies will not degrade you in the eyes of your wife. On the contrary, they will elevate you in her eyes, and she will respect you for it. Do not give in to the temptation to brazenly justify everything you do, just because you did it. Be big enough to apologize. The glow on your wife's face will be your reward.

— *10* —

Hammers and Screwdrivers

My dear son,

Did I tell you about the conference I attended in Punta del Este? I didn't think so. All right, I'll tell you about it now.

Punta del Este is a beautiful seaside resort town in Uruguay, not very far from Buenos Aires. It has a small Jewish community that is in contact with communities of Argentina. The rabbi of Punta del Este told me he was planning a community conference on issues of *shalom bayis*, and he asked me, as the author of *Dear Daughter*, to deliver an address.

According to the rabbi, many children of the community were not doing well in school, and it was discovered that there was a strong and direct correlation between the *shalom bayis* situation at home and the performance of the children in school.

The worse the *shalom bayis,* the more likely that the children would be restless and make trouble in school.

Why were there so many *shalom bayis* problems in the community? The rabbi did a little research and arrived at the conclusion that many of the men were impatient with their wives; they could not handle having to deal with feminine logic and reactions. As a result, the rabbi decided to organize a conference for the local menfolk on the theme of patience in the home, and he wanted me to speak to the people on the subject. I accepted his invitation, but I said I preferred a round table discussion to a lecture. He agreed.

After I hung up the telephone, I wondered what it was that made the men in that community so impatient. Was it the climate? Or was it perhaps the local culture? Then I began to wonder how I could possibly get these impatient men to listen patiently to what I had to say about patience.

The Ponovezher Rav came to my rescue.

I once heard a story about the Ponovezher Rav's visit to South Africa in 1927, if I am not mistaken. The Jewish community in South Africa was mostly "white," meaning to the left religiously; they were not favorably disposed to the "black" Jews who adhered to the Agudist movement. On the eve of the Ponovezher Rav's arrival in South Africa, the local Jewish paper ran a nasty piece about him. "This man is an Agudist leader, the blackest of the black. We do not want him here in South Africa. We have enough of our own blacks!"

This type of advance publicity did not intimidate the Ponovezher Rav. He spent his first Shabbos in one of the largest shuls in Johannesburg. Friday night, he asked the *gabbai* if he could address the congregation for three minutes. The *gabbai,* who had not even considered allowing him to speak, especially after the article in the paper, was taken aback by this unusual request. How could he refuse this distinguished rabbi just three minutes of time with the congregation? So the *gabbai* gave his permission, and the Ponovozher Rav went up to the *bimah.*

"A great historical event took place on this date in 1652, exactly two hundred and seventy-five years ago. A gentleman named Jan van Riebeeck disembarked from a Dutch ship at the Cape of Good Hope and became the first white man among millions of black people. Today, my good friends, we have had a complete turnabout. Standing before you, I am the only 'black' Jew among thousands of 'white' Jews."

The people were charmed and amused by the Ponovezher Rav's clever witticism, and they asked him to continue to speak. He went on to deliver a wonderful speech and to capture the hearts of the local community.

Following his example, I had to find some kind of opening that would disarm them and get by their natural resistance to the subject under discussion. I thought of something, and it worked!

"Gentlemen," I began, "how many of you have heard about the latest social movement? It is called Men's Lib."

There was a brief moment of silence, and then a burst of excitement.

"It's about time!" a young man shouted. "I never heard of this movement, but it's an idea whose time has come. Where do I sign up?"

"Great idea, Rabbi!" exclaimed another fellow as he got to his feet. "I'm all for it. You know, from the minute we got engaged, our rabbis and counselors keep telling us how patient we have to be with the women, who are so sensitive and delicate. They want us to serve the queen twenty-four hours a day. What are we? Slaves? The women have all the rights, and we have all the obligations. Now tell me, is that fair? Three cheers for Men's Lib!"

By this time, the place was rolling with laughter. Men were slapping each other on the back and speaking all at once.

"Rabbi, I have a suggestion," said a middle-aged fellow. "I make a motion that we should reinstitute Haman's Law. You know, that 'each man should rule in his own home and speak his own language.' How's that for Men's Lib? Now that would be some liberation, wouldn't it, guys?"

He was rewarded with loud applause and cheers.

"I second the motion," shouted one man.

"Me, too," shouted a number of others.

The mood was festive and relaxed.

"My friends," I said. "This is an excellent idea, and I want to propose the wording for the new law. It goes as follows: 'Every man shall have the right to do anything in order to have his wishes fulfilled.' What do you think of that?"

"Wonderful!"

"Perfect!"

"Exactly right!"

"Fine," I said. "We are making progress, but let's consider for a moment. All right, let us say you now have the right to do anything in order to have your wishes fulfilled, so what will you do? What can you do to have your wishes fulfilled? Will force and coercion bring you the fulfillment of your wishes?"

Understanding was dawning in their eyes. They realized that I had maneuvered them in a certain direction, but the spirit was so convivial that they did not seem to mind. They sat forward and listened to what would come next.

"I want to quote to you," I said, "from a letter Rav Chaim Volozhiner, a *talmid* of the Vilna Gaon, wrote to his grandson. In it, he offered a special pearl of wisdom which applies to each and every one of us in just about every aspect of our lives. 'A person is more likely to attain his desires through patience,' wrote Rav Chaim Volozhiner, 'than through the exertion of all the force in the world.'"

I repeated this sentence again and again in the traditional Mussar tune until it sank deeply into their consciousness. Then I continued.

"Imagine you have a beautiful box of lacquered wood, and the lid is closed tightly and secured with many small screws. You want to open the box and take the delicate treasure concealed inside. You pull at the lid, but it does not open. You shake the box and bang it on the table. It does not help. You could bring a big hammer and force the box open, but in the process, you would only smash the box and destroy the treasure within. What you need is a simple little screwdriver. Then you can unscrew the small screws one by one until the lid comes loose, and you can open the box without causing any damage.

"My friends, I have just presented you with 'Rav Chaim Volozhiner's Screwdriver,' the perfect tool that will bring you the fulfillment of your wishes in your marriage. It is called patience. With patience, you can open your spouse's heart so that she will rush to fulfill your wishes. It cannot necessarily be done quickly, but with patience — another kind word, another thoughtful gesture, another considerate act — you can be sure that you will open her heart to you. You will get nowhere by hammering away — only by patience.

"Now we have achieved a deeper understanding of the Men's Bill of Rights we were all promoting. We have the right to do anything to gain the fulfillment of our wishes. Yes, we have the right to be patient, because that is how we will get what we want."

My dear son, you would have enjoyed being at the conference in Punta del Este. The people really responded. I had made them think.

Now that I had opened their minds, I told them another story. Can you guess about what? Exactly! About my childhood in Buenos Aires. How did you know?

When I was little, we lived in a section of Buenos Aires that was mostly non-Jewish. As for Orthodox Jews, we were practically the only ones. Nonetheless, the neighbors all respected our family and held us in high esteem.

One day, my mother was straightening up the dining room and she discovered a mouse. My mother was absolutely terrified of mice. She could not call my father to help, because he was away at work, and she became frantic.

"Quickly," she said to me, straining to control her rising hysteria, "run across the street to the grocery. Ask the owner to come here and help me."

In a flash, I was out of the house and across the street.

"Please come quickly," I said to the grocer. "My mother needs help."

"What's the matter, young fellow?" he said.

"There's a mouse in our dining room!"

The grocer threw back his head and laughed. "You must be joking, right?"

"No, sir," I said. "We need help with the mouse. My mother is afraid."

He laughed again and slapped his thigh. "Go home and tell your mother, my young friend, that she need not be afraid. It's only a little mouse. It cannot hurt her. She's much bigger than the mouse."

Disappointed, I went home to report to my mother of the failure of my mission. My mother was beside herself. The mouse was still running around the dining room, and she was terrified. Without another word, she ran across the street and disappeared into the grocery. Moments later, she reappeared with the grocer right behind her with a large broom in his hand. The grocer chased the mouse around the dining room with his broom until he finally got rid of it.

How do you understand this story? How come the grocer laughed and laughed when I told him about the mouse, but came immediately when my mother asked him to come? Why did he leave his business unattended to go chase a mouse? Why didn't he tell her that the mouse was so little and couldn't do anything to her anyway, just as he had told me?

Do you know why? Because he saw her predicament with his own eyes. Once he saw that she was genuinely terrified, he realized that he had to help her. At that moment, all the advice in the world would have been pointless. Sure, it makes sense that a mouse cannot hurt you — but at that moment, it was irrelevant. The logic was not important.

Sometimes, a man is impatient with his wife because he considers what she wants illogical. The same holds true for a wife with her husband. However, if they would only have the patience to consider the other one's predicament, it would shine a spotlight on the emotions; it would create a deep sympathy that would result in a serene and loving home.

It is not easy to be patient but, with time and effort, it can be done. I had never considered myself an impatient person but, when I first got married, I was surprised to learn that I had a long way to go in mastering patience. To be honest, the daily tests and challenges of married life are great teachers. If we face them with a smile and a sincere desire to grow, we are rewarded with the key to the fulfillment of our wishes.

My dear son,

I have to tell you one more thing that happened at that conference in Punta del Este. After it was over, a middle-aged man came over to me and said he wanted to talk to me in private. We found a quiet corner and settled into armchairs.

"Rabbi, I liked what you said about patience," he began, "but it seems to me that this relates to young people just starting down the road of marriage. They're young. They're learning new things. It can work. Doesn't the Mishnah say that the things you learn when you're young are as if they are written on a piece of paper, or something like that? But what about me? I'm in my middle years, and I've been impatient all my life. It's part of me, part of my personality. There's really nothing I can do about it. So maybe you can do me favor? Could you speak to my wife and convince her to accept my impatience and adjust to it?"

"Just wait a minute," I said. "I disagree with you. Tell me, did you ever ride on a bus in the express bus lane, during rush hour traffic? I've done it, and it's an interesting experience. You're sitting high up, and you can see into the cars that you are passing. Hundreds of cars sitting in bumper to bumper traffic, and you can study the faces of the drivers as you pass them. I noticed that when there is an accident holding up traffic, the drivers are angry and impatient. But when it is just normal traffic congestion, the drivers appear calm and relaxed. Why do you think this is so?"

The man scratched his chin for a moment.

"Maybe it is because traffic congestion is expected," he said, "while an accident is unexpected."

"Excellent!" I said. "I think you've hit the nail on the head. When you anticipate a situation, you are prepared for it and you stay calm. When a situation takes you by surprise, it upsets you. Drivers who know that they will have to face traffic, that there are no side roads to circumvent the traffic, will come to terms with it. Drivers who are expecting a quick and easy drive are much more likely to feel frustrated when they encounter traffic. That tells us something important about human nature. A person's reaction depends on the situation. A person who has plenty to eat and is not in desperate need of money will feel exhausted and frustrated by hard manual labor. On the other hand, a person who is hungry and needs the money will be invigorated by a well-paying job, even if it involves hard manual labor.

"You, my friend, have spent decades running away from patience in your marriage. You are always looking for those little side roads that will let you avoid the need for patience. Little side roads, like asking me to convince your wife to adjust to your impatience — but you are living a mistake. Patience in marriage is unavoidable. Once you face up to the truth, you will become like those calm and relaxed drivers who know they will not be able to get through the traffic so quickly. You will discover that being patient will not exhaust or frustrate you. It will make you happy.

"You know, a person who has been smoking for fifty years because he believes it is harmless will find it hard to stop smoking. No, he will find it practically impossible to stop smoking. However, show him a pair of black lungs, proof that smoking can kill him, he will find it much easier to stop. Millions have.

"My friend, it is time for you to acknowledge your mistake and get control of your life. You will take pride in your ability to control your emotions, and you will savor the pleasures of a serene home."

You know, my son, on one of my visits to Argentina I met a Jew who was divorced and happily remarried. He had some questions about the education of his children, and he wanted my advice.

In the course of the conversation, I asked him, "Why did you divorce your first wife?"

"I just had no patience for her," he said. "I couldn't deal with her."

"I see. And now you are happily married?"

"Oh yes. Very much so."

"So is your second wife opposite in character to your first wife?"

"No. Not at all. You can't imagine how much patience I need to deal with her."

"I don't understand," I said. "Why are you able to be so much more patient with this wife than you were with your first wife?"

He smiled and shrugged. "You learn from your mistakes."

My dear son,

I want to remind you about the time we spent Shabbos near the hospital in a tenth-floor apartment. You were quite young then, but I'm sure you remember it. We were climbing the stairs to the apartment, and you were grumbling and complaining about how your feet hurt. I then started telling you amusing stories, and pretty soon you were laughing and enjoying yourself. You completely forgot your aching feet.

When we reached the ninth floor, I suddenly realized that I did not have the Shabbos belt with the key. We would have to go all the way down to get it and climb all the way back up to the apartment. How could I tell you this awful news?

Do you remember what I did? I started laughing really hard. "I just thought of the funniest thing," I gasped in between peals of laughter.

"Tell me," you begged. "Please tell me."

"It's funnier than any of the stories I already told you," I said and broke down laughing again.

"Please, please, tell me."

"All right," I said. "We don't have the Shabbos belt with the key to the apartment. We have to go all the way back down to get it."

You looked at me, and I looked at you, and then we both started laughing so hard that we could not stop. After we caught our breath, we went down the stairs, got the key and came back up, and you were fine. No complaints, no grumbles. Why? Because our lighthearted banter had put you in a good mood and had given you a positive attitude to the situation.

This is an important lesson for life. If you have a positive attitude, you can accomplish the most difficult and strenuous tasks, and you can have fun while you're doing it.

The patience required in a successful marriage, believe me, is much more strenuous than climbing ten flights of stairs twice. People come from different backgrounds, they have different natures, different outlooks, different upbringings, and everything has to mesh together smoothly. It is not an easy thing, but a positive attitude can make it easier and more enjoyable. Humor always helps a little in building patience, but it is far from the whole answer.

The most important thing is to appreciate the benefits of patience and to understand, with your whole heart, that it is really worthwhile.

One time, when I was a youngster in Argentina, I wanted very much to go to an extremely popular vacation spot called Mar del Plata. The demand was so great that we had to wait in line for bus tickets. Do you know how long I waited in line? All night! That's right, I stood in line the entire night. And listen to this, the people on line were chatting all night, and I discovered that I was standing next to a well-known soccer star. He knew how beautiful it is in Mar del Plata, and even he considered it worth his while to stand in line all night, just to get there.

Today, our pampered young people have everything handed to them on silver platters. Everything comes so easily that they have no appreciation for what they have. As such, they naturally develop negative attitudes towards anything that requires patience.

I once saw something that I would not have believed if I had not seen it with my own eyes. I was in a gas station, and I saw a young man, a *bachur*, drive in. He looked like he was going on a trip. He went into the convenience mart and came out with a quart of orange juice. He then took a drink and threw the rest into the garbage.

"Excuse me," I said to him. "Why are you throwing the orange juice into the garbage? It's practically full."

"I know," he said. "But what am I supposed to do? Hold the container in my hand for a full hour? If I put it down, it will spill."

So tell me, is this young man prepared to deal patiently with the normal stresses and challenges of marriage? Will he be able to exert himself?

Rabbeinu Yonah makes this point on the *passuk* in *Mishlei* (14:4), "*B'ein alafim aivus bar.* Without the oxen, the bin is bare." Rabbeinu Yonah elaborates on this parable. He writes that a farmer cleans his stable when the oxen are away. Then he brings them back, and they soil it again. Why does he do it? He does it because he understands that his oxen bring him far more benefit than trouble. He sees the total picture, and that makes all the difference.

We used to have a neighbor, a very fine woman who was also kind and helpful to our family. Do you remember the brown rocking chair that we had in our living room? She had wanted to give it to us as a gift, but we would not accept it, so she sold it to us for a dollar.

This woman had a dog that was always with her; you never saw her without her dog. When your older sister was born, we set up the apartment beautifully for the *kiddush*, as you can well imagine. Our neighbor came over to see the baby and, as usual, her dog was with her. Well, how should I put this? The dog had an accident in the middle of the floor. The women who worked so hard to prepare the *kiddush* began screaming hysterically but, for us who appreciated the goodness of our neighbor, there was no cause for hysteria. We patiently cleaned up and went on.

My son, the issues in a marriage that call for patience arise from the differences between husband and wife. A woman is opposite in nature to a man, but that is why they complement each other so perfectly. That is the source of the joy and happiness in marriage, the perfect union between the opposites. If you understand this and take it to heart, if you appreciate the benefits you will derive from your marriage, then you will surely find the patience to work through the issues successfully.

∽

My dear son,

A final thought on patience. You will not learn patience in one day, nor in one week. It will be a gradual process, and the longer you work at it, the more successful you will be.

Rav Sholom Schwadron once told the following story in the Lakewood Yeshivah. A woman with a serious problem came to the Chazon Ish for a *berachah*. The Chazon Ish listened to her, but he remained silent. The woman pleaded with him again and again, and still, he remained silent.

When the woman persisted, one of the men standing there said to her, "Don't you see that he does not want to answer you?"

The Chazon Ish gave the man a sharp look and said, "Whom did she come to see, you or me? Why are you speaking for me?"

Later, the Chazon Ish explained to the man why he had rebuked him so sharply. "While she was asking me for a *berachah*," he said, "she was immersed in *emunas chachamim*, trust in the Sages, and growing by the minute. Then you stopped her!"

The same applies to patience. When you work on your patience, you grow by the minute. You become a better, more patient person.

Let me finish with a brief story. I was going to a *chasunah* in New York, and I got a ride with the *chassan's* friend, a young man who had recently gotten married. He arranged to pick me up last before leaving Lakewood.

This young man was always a strictly punctual fellow, and I expected him to be on time. This time, he arrived at my house late. He apologized and explained that we would still have to go back to pick up his wife who was not yet ready. She would be waiting for us on the sidewalk.

We drove to the other side of town, where he lived. What should I tell you? There was no one on the sidewalk when we got there. I could see the extreme frustration on his face. I thought to myself that it must be a real ordeal for a punctual fellow like him to have a wife who is not punctual.

He controlled himself. He gave a light tap on the horn when, in earlier days, he would have leaned on the horn. Another minute passed, and still no one came out. I saw the astonishment on his face. How could this be? He had gone to pick me up and come all the way back, and still she wasn't ready? In earlier days, he would have stormed out of the car and made a scene, but not now. What did he do? He started to sing one soft and gentle tune after another.

I was impressed. He was working on his patience — and succeeding!

Then his wife came out, and their smiles were so sweet that all the patient waiting had been worthwhile. I remember thinking to myself that, if she had waited a few more minutes more, he would have progressed even further in the development of his patience.

That is life. One long process of growth. And it all begins with *bechirah*, with a choice of free will. If you choose to go down this path, as you absolutely must if you want to have a successful marriage, you will control your emotions rather than having your emotions control you.

Rav Aharon Kotler's *rebbetzin* said during her husband's *shivah*, "When we first got married, I had to adapt to my husband's sharpness. In later years, I had to adapt to his patience."

— *11* —

*A Cool Breeze
on a Hot Day*

My dear son,

When I was a youngster in high school in Buenos Aires, I once went to a government office to fill out some papers. It was a tedious business, and I expected an hour of drudgery and boredom. After filling out one form, I showed it to one of the clerks in the office, for approval.

The clerk glanced through the form and said, "You did it right and, by the way, you have a really nice handwriting." The comment was unexpected, and it gave me a feeling of sheer delight. After that, I found the rest of the time I spent in the office filling out forms strangely enjoyable.

I was intrigued by the transformative power of a few words of mild praise and, when I returned to school, I discussed it with my classmates. Why do people give praise? What is their motivation?

After an animated half-hour, my classmates agreed that praise was really nothing more than simple flattery. It is a way of getting something from other people ∇ the tools of a salesman. People who have a natural flair for sales in all of its many forms are more likely to praise others instinctively, while ordinary people only give praise on those rare occasions when they expect something in return.

A short while later, my father's friend, Dovid Cohen, visited Buenos Aires. Mr. Cohen was a successful community leader, a distinguished and highly respected individual who was far removed from flattery. Nonetheless, he praised people constantly, lavishly and with such dignity that they hung on to his every word and rushed to do his bidding.

One time, I had an opportunity to exchange a few words in private with Mr. Cohen, and I brought up the issue of praise. "I was wondering why people praise other people. I discussed this with my classmates, and we reached the conclusion that praise was really nothing more than flattery. Nevertheless, I see how you give so much praise, and you are clearly not a flatterer. Maybe you can explain it to me."

"First of all," said Mr. Cohen, "I don't understand why you would seek an answer to such a serious question by asking your classmates. Why not your father? You have a wonderful father. You should look to him for your answers. Right now, however, I will give you an answer.

"When I was a young boy, I got on a bus and took a seat by the window. As the bus was about to leave, I saw a fellow Jew running to catch the bus, but I didn't say anything to the driver. I just sat there and watched as the man missed the bus. My father found out about this, but he didn't say anything to me, right away.

"The next Shabbos afternoon, he offered to learn with me a very interesting Gemara (*Kesubos* 16). The Gemara discusses what you should say when your friend purchases something that you find unappealing. For instance, he bought a new car that you consider ugly. Should you praise his new purchases or should you just be quiet? The Gemara concludes that you are obligated to praise it, in order to 'fulfill the wishes of every Jew.'

"So my father asked me, 'Why should a person have to fulfill everyone's wishes?'

"I thought for a moment and said, 'You taught me, Father, that a Jew has to work very hard to do *chessed* with others. I would say that this is part of the obligation of *chessed*.'

"My father smiled. 'Beautiful,' he said. 'But the *Shitah Mekubetzes* says otherwise. He says it is an obligation of *derech eretz*, respect. To praise someone's purchases is to show him respect, and we are required to respect all people.'

"'It seems to me,' I said, 'that fulfilling everyone's wishes is a hard thing that can only be expected from people who are on a very high spiritual level.'

"'Not so,' said my father. 'If fulfilling another person's wish requires a great deal of effort, it is certainly also a great act of *chessed*, which ordinary people cannot really be expected to do. However, if it requires no effort, everyone is obligated to do it.' My father's face suddenly clouded, and his eyes flashed with anger. 'And anyone who doesn't help another person where it requires no effort is worse than a stinking carcass in the road!'

"At that moment, I understood exactly what my father was saying, and the source of his anger. He knew about the man who had missed the bus. It would have been easy for me to call out to the driver, 'Wait a minute! Someone's running for the bus!' ∇ but I didn't. I said nothing, and in doing so, I disrespected the man who was running for the bus, as if I had spit in his face. From that day on, I became more sensitive to other people. I try my best to show everyone respect, and I have found that praising people is one of the most effective ways of showing respect, just as the *Shitah Mekubetzes* says on that Gemara.

"I once walked into a shul and saw an old man with a worried look on his face, so I said to him, 'Excuse me, did you eat an extra bowl of Cheerios this morning? You have such a healthy look!' The man looked up, surprised. Then his face broke into an incandescent smile, and every trace of his earlier worry was gone. He thanked me profusely for my simple comment. Later, I discovered that the man had been having some pains, and his imagination was conjuring up all the worst case scenarios. My few words of praise had put him in a good mood and dispelled all his distressing thoughts. Look what a few words of praise can do! If you have any respect for other people and you can do so much for them with a few simple words of praise, how can you not praise people?

"In addition, remember for the future; don't go to your classmates for answers to this kind of philosophical question. Go to your father."

These words made a very deep impression on me. I think that every *chassan* should be required to learn this Gemara before his wedding, because praise is such an important factor in a marriage.

You know, a politician running for office comes to a community and makes a speech. The next day, he runs to get the newspapers to see what kind of impression he made. He wants to see words of praise. Now tell me, why does he want that praise? Because he wants honor? To a certain extent, that is true, but it is not the main thing. He needs the praise for his own self-esteem. He needs the validation. He needs to know that he came across to the people in a positive way and that he is being successful in his campaign.

A wife needs her husband's praise for similar reasons.

The Chazon Ish writes in one of his letters, "The nature of a woman is to enjoy finding favor with her husband. She looks to him for approval."

It is very important for a woman to please her husband, and to win his favor and approval. Therefore, when her husband praises her, it is her greatest joy and delight. When he praises her, she feels validated and, above all, successful. Believe me, she enjoys the praise more than the politician enjoys all the complimentary articles in the newspapers.

Think about it. One little word of praise, said with sincerity, can bring joy and blessing to your home. One little word!

∽

My dear son,

I remember when you made your first *siyum*. It was an exciting event for our family. Your mother wrote a poem in honor of the occasion and gave it to you. I remember how moved you were by the poem. You kept pulling it out and reading it again and again; you couldn't stop talking about it.

I also remember you coming home one day and complaining that your math teacher kept praising you and praising you all the time. You didn't like it; it made you feel uncomfortable.

Tell me, what was the difference between the two? Were you a person who likes praise or were you not such a person?

This is not such a difficult question. I'm sure you can give me the answer, but I would like to explain it in some detail.

Poetry, writes the Chazon Ish, is the art of conveying those deep feelings that cannot be expressed in words alone. That is the special power of poems. They can reach deep inside your heart and bring out the emotions that would otherwise remain unexpressed.

You know, of course, that *Shir HaShirim,* Hashem's love song to the Jewish people and one of the most beautiful poems ever written, is considered *kodesh kodashim,* the holiest of the holy. But here is something you may not have heard yet. The *Midrash Tanchuma* in *Parashas Tetzaveh* says that no day was as great as the day that Shir Hashirim was given to the Jewish people. Why? asks the Midrash. What was so special about that day? The Midrash answers, "Look how the A-mighty praises the Jewish people. He says, 'You are beautiful, my beloved. You are beautiful with your good deeds.'"

So the greatness of *Shir HaShirim* lies in Hashem praising the Jewish people. Can you understand such a thing? Does this praise of the Jewish people for their good deeds explain why *Shir HaShirim* is holier than all the other *sefarim* in *kesuvim,* the Writings portion of the Torah?

I'm sure you are as puzzled as I was when I first saw this Midrash. But do you know why we are puzzled? It is because we do not appreciate the meaning and the value of praise.

Tanna D'vei Eliyahu (17) explains that, through His praises, the Almighty expresses His joy and His deep love for the Jewish people. So you see, *Shir HaShirim* is not just praise. It is the embodiment of the Divine love for the Jewish people. And when we see His love for us expressed, our hearts respond with love for Him and His Torah. That is what makes *Shir HaShirim kodesh kodashim.* That is why the day it was given to the Jewish people is one of the most important days in the history of the world.

When your mother wrote you that poem, you saw in its lines the depth and breadth of your mother's love for you, and it touched your heart. It was so dear and precious to you that you could not get enough of it. On the other hand, when your teacher routinely doles out lavish praise, you know there is no great love behind it. It is like a disembodied recorded message that comes on when you give a certain answer. That is why it made you uncomfortable. It did not have any emotional depth.

The A-mighty blessed husband and wife with an endless love that is deeply engraved in their hearts, a love that grows stronger every day as it responds to the love of the other. It is said of Rav Akiva Eiger that, when his wife passed away, he became deathly ill and almost died himself. How could he go on living when the heart that was fused with his had been torn away?

This love, this endless love that fires and inspires the relationship, is expressed by words of praise, just as the Almighty's love for the Jewish people was expressed by words of praise. When you praise your wife, her personal qualities, her deeds, her efforts, her accomplishments, your words will be like a poem carrying a message of the deepest love. You do not have to be a poet. You do not have to use colorful language. As long as they come from your heart, your words will refresh her like a cool breeze on a hot day.

You know, there used to be a custom in *yeshivos* that a new *chassan* would give out cigarettes to his friends, and they would wish him *mazel tov*. Of course, now that we know the herm cigarettes cause, we do not see it so much. Anyway, what used to happen was that the friends would give the *chassan* a big hug and wish him a hearty *mazel tov*, then they would take their cigarettes. Sometimes, a fellow just wanted a cigarette, so he would walk over, mumble a quick *mazel tov*, take his cigarette and leave. So tell me, what value does such a *mazel tov* have?

A husband who mumbles a few obligatory words of praise to his wife after she has exerted herself on his behalf, and then is out the door, has really not expressed any love with his words of praise. They are just empty words. I can assure you that his wife will not accept them like a cool breeze on a hot day. She will more likely find them annoying, just as you found that math teacher's praise bothersome.

In order to give genuine praise, you have to focus on what your wife has done, appreciate it and show your recognition. If she prepares a new dish for you, praise it and ask for a second helping. She will love the recognition and consider it the greatest praise.

It is well known that the Chafetz Chaim never attributed any importance to the taste of food. He would never say that a certain food is good or delicious. Nonetheless, when his *rebbetzin* prepared a new dish for him, he found a way to give her praise and recognition. He would taste the food and then he would say, "Hmm. This is an interesting dish." Those words undoubtedly touched her heart and made her feel wonderful.

Before I go, just a small tip on praise. People who have flaws, especially physical flaws, are very aware of them, and they are sensitive. A husband, or anyone else for that matter, should not give praise that belies those flaws. Such praise is insincere and false; it will only cause hurt. Instead, he should praise her real virtues and not talk about the flaws. If she has a limp and he praises her beautiful eyes, she will feel good. This, too, you can derive from that Gemara in *Kesubos* we mentioned before. Look it up.

My dear son,

In your last letter, you asked for my advice for a friend of yours, who found it difficult to praise his wife. He claims that his wife does ten things wrong for every one thing she does right, so how is he supposed to praise her? Praise is supposed to come from the happiness in his heart, and all he feels is frustration. He claims he is only human, and he is upset. I think that is basically all the information you gave me, right?

First of all, I have to tell you that I cannot speak directly to this young man's problems. I don't know him. People sometimes come to me for advice and we speak for hours before I can begin to figure out what they are all about. So how can you expect me to give advice on such a delicate matter to a young man whom I have never met?

Instead, let's talk about this issue in general terms, all right?

Remember I wrote to you about a friend of mine who is a master *rebbi*? Well, let me tell you about another of his experiences.

One day, another *rebbi* was sitting in the back of the room and observing my friend's class, in order to learn from his methods and techniques. During class, one of the boys started to act up. The *rebbi* gave him a sharp look. It didn't help. The mischief continued. The *rebbi* warned him that he would have to punish him. The boy became upset. He claimed it was not his fault, and that others were really doing whatever it was. He also lashed out at the *rebbi* in very disrespectful, even shocking, language. The *rebbi* told him he was punished and would have to remain in detention after class.

The lesson resumed, and the *rebbi* asked this same boy a question he knew the boy could answer. As expected, the boy gave the correct answer. The *rebbi* praised him lavishly and even gave him a kiss.

After class, the visiting *rebbi* asked him, "Weren't you hurt by the language that boy used?"

"Of course I was," he replied. "What do you think, that I'm made of stone?"

"So how could you praise and even kiss him?"

"I'm not a policeman or a judge, and the boy is not a criminal. I'm a *rebbi*, and my job is to help the child, to teach him, to awaken and reinforce his good traits. The Gemara says that *smol merachek veyemin mekarev*, push him away with the left hand and draw him near with the right hand. A child is fragile and tender so when we push him away we use the weaker left hand, but we use the strong right hand to draw the child near. I punished him for his remarks, but I shower him with love for his accomplishments. You will see, tomorrow he will be an angel in my class."

This, my son, is the approach your friend should take with his wife. He should bring her closer with his right hand and praise her lavishly where she deserves it. If he does this, her self-esteem will grow and the relationship will flourish. Then he will see that, little by little, using kindness and not harsh criticism, all those things he claims she does wrong will gradually become fewer and fewer.

It will no doubt take an effort on his part, a serious effort, but if he understands her nature and cares about their relationship, he will be able to do it. If his praise is wholehearted and sincere, he will be successful.

I remember overhearing a conversation you were having on the telephone with one of your friends when you were a *chassan*. You were standing in the living room and saying, "What? I should call my father-in-law *Tatty*? . . . I can't do that. For me, there is only one *Tatty* . . . Why, I hardly know my father-in-law. How can I call him *Tatty*? . . . I know that my father-in-law is a wonderful person, but my emotions won't let me call him *Tatty*. . . You really think it is important for the relationship with him? . . . You think it will mean a lot to my *kallah*? . . . All right, I'll do it. From now on, he is *Tatty*."

You showed real maturity, my son. In the beginning of the conversation you emotions were in turmoil, but then you looked at it logically and gained control. You made the right decision.

Your friend should learn from you. He should gain control of his emotions and focus on what is best for his relationship. If he does that, he will have no trouble praising her with full sincerity.

— *12* —

*Truthful
Denials*

My dear son,

There seems to be a not uncommon complaint among men that their wives can be less than fully truthful. More than one husband has complained to me that his wife almost never admits to wrongdoing, even if there is no question that she is responsible. The first thing that comes out of her mouth is a denial.

This is a serious complaint. Trust is the foundation of every relationship. So how is a husband supposed to deal with a wife who lies?

So let's think about this. What are these wives who respond to their husbands with denials of wrongdoing? Are they liars? Are they dishonest people who could not be trusted in sensitive jobs?

I don't think so. Of course, there are some people, among both men and women, who are simply unscrupulous liars.

However, most of these women, about whose reflexive denials their husbands complain, are good and decent people. It is only in their relationships with their husbands that they somehow feel constrained to offer denials, even if they are less than truthful.

Let me explain.

In the Torah, we find that when the *malachim* told Avraham that his elderly wife Sarah would give birth to a son, "she laughed inside." Then Avraham confronted her and asked, "Why did you laugh?", and how did Sarah respond? She denied it!

Now, was Sarah a truthful person or a liar, Heaven forbid?

The *Rivash* explains that Sarah was certainly a most truthful person. During all the many years of their married life, Avraham had never heard one lie from her, and now, suddenly, she abandons truthfulness? It cannot be. How then do we explain her denial? This denial, he points out, did not result from a lack of truthfulness. It was an instinctive reaction caused by her feminine nature.

Let us imagine a loyal minister of a king, a man who feared and revered his royal sovereign and served him faithfully for his entire life. Then something happened. He made a mistake and incurred the displeasure of the king. The king rebuked him sharply and asked him what had happened. The minister was so devoted to the king and so mortified by his misstep that, out of respect and reverence, he could not bring himself to utter the words of admission from his mouth. He simply could not face up to what he had done nor could he look the king in the face and speak of it.

The *Orach HaChaim* explains that Sarah had a similar relationship with Avraham. She respected and revered him and was utterly devoted to him. She had absorbed all his holy teachings, including the importance and primacy of having *bitachon*, trust in the A-mighty, and in knowing and understanding that nothing is beyond His power. And now, when she had heard the A-mighty's messengers foretell that she would have a child in her old age — she had laughed!

Sarah was mortified. How could she have exhibited such a lack of *bitachon*? How could she have betrayed the values her illustrious husband was teaching to the entire world? As such, when Avraham asked her why she laughed, she couldn't face up to what she had done, and she instinctively denied it. She was not lying. She was just overwhelmed by the magnitude of her failing. She could not bring herself to utter those horrendous words of admission but, in her facial expressions and her tone of voice, she signaled to Avraham that she had done it and pleaded for his forbearance and understanding.

Put yourself in Avraham's shoes when he hears her denial. He sees that his wife's devotion and her respect for him and his teachings are so great that she cannot bring herself to say she slipped up. He also sees in her eyes her plea for understanding. It must have been a very gratifying moment for him.

How then did he respond? Not with anger. Not with accusations. With a simple statement of fact. "No, you did laugh." He set the record straight and left it at that.

More often than not, this is what is going on when a wife responds to her husband with denials. She is not lying. On the contrary, she can be the most truthful person, but her feminine nature will not allow her to admit her failing. She is so devoted to her husband and is so thirsty for his approval and esteem that she is horrified when she slips up. Her devotion and respect for her husband make it difficult and sometimes impossible for her to admit what she has done. However, if you listen to her words carefully, you will hear the signals of truth and the pleas for understanding.

Let me tell you a story about a middle-aged engineer who made a comfortable living and had a beautiful home. Then his older brother died and left him his fortune. Overnight, the engineer became a multimillionaire. He and his wife called in an interior decorator to make their home even more beautiful, to show off their new wealth. After much discussion with the decorator, however, they decided they were satisfied with their existing décor and were not prepared to uproot everything in their middle age. Instead, they wanted the decorator to find them a stunning painting, a rare work of art, to hang on their living room wall.

A week later, the decorator took them to a gallery to see the painting she had chosen for them. It was a famous masterpiece, a winter scene in a small town, extremely expensive but worth every penny.

The engineer looked closely at the painting.

"This is not good," he said.

The decorator looked at him in shock. "What are you saying? This is a famous, almost priceless masterpiece. How can you say it is no good?"

"Look, I know this place in the painting," he said. "I grew up in that town, and I know every street, every nook and cranny. I could show you many mistakes in the painting. That building, for instance, has six floors, not seven, and the bridge across the river is further away from this park ∇ just to mention a couple."

"My dear sir," said the decorator, "this is a work of art, not an engineering diagram. The artist is not building a bridge here. He is conveying a feeling. Look at it closely for a minute or two and let it speak to you."

She waited a brief while, and then she said, "In this painting, the artist is conveying the utter coldness of a winter storm. You look at those people caught outside in the storm, and you feel like offering them a hot drink."

The engineer gave her a quizzical look. "You know, that was exactly what was going through my mind."

You see, my son, when you are admiring a work of art you have to have the proper perspective. Just because the dimensions are not accurate does not mean that it is not a work of art, or that it does not convey a message of deep truth. If you look at it from the proper perspective, you will see beyond the inaccuracies of the details and see the greater truth of the painting.

The same is true in a marriage. Even if your wife responds to you with denials that are not technically accurate, you have to see the greater picture. You have to understand the feeling and emotions that have engendered these denials. You have to recognize that they are coming from a heart full of love and respect for her husband. You have to understand that these very denials are the strongest expressions of her love.

$$\backsim$$

My dear son,

I want to explore with you another dimension of the feminine nature that has great relevance to the issue of denials. But first let me tell you a story I once heard.

There was a non-observant couple who had an only child, a son named Joey, who was a nightclub singer. Eventually, this son became a *baal teshuvah.* He gave up his job and went to learn in a yeshivah in Yerushalayim. The mother was very attached to her only child, and she yearned for the day when he would come back from Israel. In the meantime, the parents spoke to their son by telephone every Thursday afternoon; they would call him in his yeshivah and speak for a long while.

One Thursday evening, the couple went for a stroll, and they happened to pass the nightclub where their son Joey used to sing. Just then, a young man who bore a slight resemblance to their son in build and coloring came out of the nightclub.

The woman looked at him, and her eyes widened. "Joey!" she cried.

She was about to embrace him, but her husband held her back. "It's not Joey," he said to her gently.

She realized she was mistaken and apologized. The next morning, she called Israel again and told her son about her mistake.

Now, think about what happened here. Cases of mistaken identity are fairly common, but a mother will usually realize the mistake in a split second. In this case, all logic said that it could not have been her son Joey. First of all, she had just spoken to him in Israel just a few hours earlier. How could he possibly have managed to leave the yeshivah and come to America in such a short time? It was impossible. Besides, now that Joey had become a *baal teshuvah* and was learning seriously in a yeshivah, coming out of a nightclub is the last place you would expect to find him. How then could she make such a mistake?

The answer lies in the intensity of a mother's love for her children. The instant she saw the young man who resembled her son, her deep and powerful yearning for her son's return burst forth from her heart and created for her an alternate reality, and logic went right out the window. In this parallel world she had created for herself and which she now inhabited, everything was possible. Joey could be coming out of a nightclub in America just hours after he had been on the telephone in Israel, because this is what the new reality demanded.

This is how the *Tosefos HaShalem* explain Sarah's denial, "*Miharah lehakchish.* She rushed to deny it." Sarah's denial was not a white lie. The rush of her emotions, her deep chagrin at having laughed and not having had the proper *bitachon,* her devotion to her husband and her boundless respect for him, all these combined to create an alternate reality for her and, in her mind, she could not possibly have laughed, even though it had actually happened.

Had she stopped to think it through, she would have realized that she had indeed laughed, and she would not have denied it. However, in the rush of emotions her mind was transported to an alternate reality of her own making, a reality in which she could not have laughed.

This is what happens in many marriages. Sometimes the husband offers the wife a criticism about something that seems to him to be so blatantly clear and simple that there can be no argument about it. And the wife instantly replies, "That's how you see it — but I see it my way." The husband is beside himself with frustration. How is he supposed to convince her that the sky is blue, when she claims it is green?

The answer is that, at that moment, considering the play of emotions, she really does see a green sky. She is not lying or being difficult. Just like Sarah, she sees the alternate reality that her emotions have created in her mind.

— *13* —

*The Good
Guest*

My dear son,

Two men were traveling together to the Catskill Mountains on a Friday afternoon during the winter months. They got caught in a snowstorm and, for a while, it seemed they would have to make Shabbos by the roadside. Fortunately, however, they managed to pull into Kiryas Yoel, the Satmar community in Monroe, just a few minutes before sundown.

A local resident saw the two men stumble out of the car and invited them to his house for Shabbos. They accepted gratefully.

Friday night, their host seated them at his table and served them lavishly. The men ate and drank their fill and, in the glow of contentment, they went out for a stroll through the village.

"I am so impressed by our host," one of them remarked to his friend. "What a wonderful person he is! Look at the beautiful feast he prepared just for us."

"What do you mean, just for us?" asked his friend. "That is nonsense. He did not prepare anything for us. Why, he did not even know we were coming until a few minutes before Shabbos. He prepared for himself and his family. We just happened to show up and, I tell you, it's a good thing there was enough food for us as well."

So tell me, my son. Which of these two people is correct, the first or the second? You're thinking twice, because you know I have something up my sleeve, right? Well, I do.

Look up the Gemara in *Berachos* (58a), and you'll find this exact situation discussed. The Gemara contrasts the "good guest" and the "bad guest." The "good guest" is described as the one who says, "Look at what the host has done for me. Look at how much he has served me and how much he has troubled himself for my sake." The "bad guest," on the other hand, is the one who says, "What did I take from him already? He was going through all this trouble anyway on behalf of his own wife and children."

Here we are talking about our two friends stranded in Kiryas Yoel. The first gentleman would be considered the "good guest," because he appreciates what his host did for him, even though he did not know that he was coming. His friend, however, is like the "bad guest." He looks at things in a narrow-minded way; he is a harsh realist. He sees that the host was preparing for himself and his family anyway, so he doesn't see any special kindness in the hospitality of the host. On the other hand, the "good guest" has an open mind and a deep insight. He realizes that the host was preparing for himself and his family anyway, but he does appreciate that the host opened his home to him and let him share his bounty.

The Yerushalmi (*Berachos* 9:1) adds that the "good guest" gives two special blessings to the host. Clearly, the "good guest's" heartfelt appreciation and praise of the kindness of his host engenders an emotional closeness between the two.

Now think, my son. If you consider your wife's efforts on your behalf through the eyes of the "good guest," you will see clearly that she toils for you, twenty-four hours a day. Everything she does is for you, so that you should be happy and pleased. If you really appreciate her kindness and devotion, think of the emotional closeness that will result, and the blessings to her that will be forever on your lips.

Do you remember when you spoke at your sister's *sheva berachos*? Your speech was short and sweet, a paean of praise to the *kallah*. I recall that the *chassan* listened to you with moist eyes and afterward he hugged you. Why was he so touched? What did you say that he did not already know? Nothing really. But you praised his *kallah* in such a beautiful way that he immediately felt an emotional closeness to you.

Praise, my son, doesn't have to come from a third person in order to have this effect. If you praise your wife in the same way, just between the two of you, you will also feel a surge of emotional closeness, a fresh breeze of love and companionship, every single time. It does not necessarily have to be praise all the time, either. It can be a warm and sunny "thank you!" accompanied by a bright smile, or any other expression of your gratitude and appreciation. I'm sure you are wise enough to come up with a whole list.

You know, in our society the young people are sometimes not sufficiently trained in gratitude. Parents often dote on their children to the point where the children do not even realize that it is not "coming to them," and that they have to be grateful for what they receive.

A *bachur* spends years learning in yeshivah and, unless the message is constantly driven into his consciousness, he can easily forget that he has to be grateful to the yeshivah for everything it does for him, both spiritually and materially. He can tell himself that it is important for the yeshivah to provide good conditions, if it wants to maintain its status as a good yeshivah. In other words, he can so easily be a "bad guest."

Were he a "good guest," he would be forever grateful to his parents for paying the tuition and to his *rosh yeshivah* for carrying the burden of the yeshivah on his shoulders, and to the cook and the kitchen staff for preparing and serving the meals every day, and to the custodial staff for keeping the halls, bathrooms and grounds neat and clean. Someone has to reinforce these thoughts in his mind, and it is not always done.

I think your mother and I did a good job raising you to appreciate everything that is done for you and to express your gratitude, but what about those boys who are not brought up this way? What happens when such a boy reaches marriageable age? What happens when he gets married? In his mind, he may just have exchanged one building for another. Before it was the yeshivah, and now it is his apartment. Just as he took everything for granted there, he takes everything for granted here. He accepts everything as if it is coming to him, without a feeling of gratitude and without the courtesy of a thank you.

Believe me, he will learn quickly enough. The boys in the yeshivah also expressed their gratitude, from time to time, by giving the cook a present ∇ but it is not enough. He has to become a "good guest" in his own home. He has to engender in his heart a deep appreciation for everything his wife does for him ∇ which is literally everything ∇ and he has to show his appreciation, with expressions of gratitude and blessings. Only then will he enjoy the constant emotional closeness and a relationship that deepens all the time.

A woman once called me up to ask my advice about her husband. She was in tears and could barely get the words out. Her husband was particularly fond of a particular type of chocolate cake and of certain fancy cookies. She went out and got all the ingredients and spent hours preparing the cake and the cookies. Her husband ate some of the cookies and thanked her for them, but he didn't touch the cake or say a word about it. She was beside herself. Later, the husband called me and said he could not understand his wife. He had thanked her so nicely for the cookies, and she was not satisfied.

You see? He was a typical "bad guest." He saw everything narrowly from his own perspective. He thanked her for what he ate, but he was completely insensitive to what she had done for him. Had he been a "good guest," he would have told her that, right now, he could only eat a few cookies, but he was touched by everything she went through to make him such a beautiful cake. In addition, if he had been a real *mentsch*, he would have taken a tiny sliver of the cake, even if he did not want any right then, and he would have praised her for a cake that has the *taam* of Gan Eden, a true taste of paradise. And you know something? Had he done that, he would have experienced paradise in his home, instead of a wife in tears.

When I was a child in public school in Argentina, I had to do a book report on *Uncle Tom's Cabin,* a book about the suffering of slaves in America before the Civil War. It told the story of a mother who was sold to one slave owner and her child to another, like insensate pieces of property. In my research, I discovered that President Lincoln credited this book with setting off the Civil War.

How could such a thing be? This book did not tell people anything they did not know before. If so, how could it have had such a major impact? Do you know the answer? Because people had not related to the situation on a human level. They knew that the slaves were considered and treated like property, but it was all abstract. Then they read this book, and they saw the human tragedy. They felt the pain and the suffering, and they realized that such a thing could not be allowed to continue.

At the root of it, this is the difference between the "good guest" and the "bad guest." The "bad guest" relates to his host in an abstract way. He realizes that the host is doing things for him, but he does not connect on the human level. He does not feel the emotions of the host. The "good guest," however, sees deeply. He recognizes the deep wellsprings of kindness in his host's heart, and he responds in the same way.

My son, if a book can change the attitude of an entire country, surely the wise words of the Gemara can transform your home into a paradise.

$$— 14 —$$

The Winning Argument

My dear son,

When I was a child in Argentina, I was a soccer fan. Do you know how I became a soccer fan? I had a teacher in public school who was a rabid soccer fan. Every Monday, we could tell by his behavior what Boca, his favorite soccer team, had done the day before. If they had won on Sunday, he would come to school in an expansive mood, jolly and friendly to all the students. On the other hand, if they lost on Sunday, watch out! He would come to school in a black mood, and woe to the student who got in his way.

Therefore, every Sunday night, I would listen to the radio to hear the scores in order to know what to expect the next day from our volatile teacher. As time went on, I actually became a soccer fan, so I understand what sports are all about. I heard in the name of a certain very old *gadol* who grew up in America that, even today, every time he hears the Yankees mentioned, he feels a twinge in his heart; the *yetzer hara* is still there. As for myself, baseball means nothing to me, but soccer? That is a different story. Whenever I pass by a field where young boys are kicking a soccer ball, I have a strong *yetzer hara* to stop and watch the game.

What is it about sports that makes it so attractive to fans? Do you remember when we read about the Super Bowl being played in a northern city, during in a tremendous blizzard? Thousands upon thousands of fans showed up at the stadium with blankets and Thermoses, to watch the game in person! All those people could have just as easily stayed at home and watched the game in full color in the comforts of a warm, cozy living room, yet they braved the elements to go to the stadium. Why? What was so important that it made the miserable ordeal of shivering in frigid weather worthwhile?

I think the answer is well-known to most American sports fans. They want to be involved. They get a vicarious pleasure out of watching their team play. When their team plays, it is as if they themselves are on the field, scoring those touchdowns and making those brilliant defensive moves. Sitting in their living rooms, however, they will not feel involved. They have to be there, sharing the experience, shivering in the freezing cold, connecting with the crowd and the players, cheering and screaming until their lungs are about to burst. Then they can feel that when their team has won, they too, in a sense, have won. And every person loves to feel victorious. Every person loves to be a winner.

My teacher in Buenos Aires, rabid soccer fan that he was, was ready to ruin half his life, to sour his relationship with his students, when his team was playing poorly. All this just to be able to delude himself into thinking that he was a winner.

There was a member of our *shul* in Argentina named Reb Shlomo who was widely known as a pious man. He was also famous for always performing the *mitzvah* of *kiddush lavanah* meticulously. We all looked up to him and admired him greatly.

One Shabbos, just as we were concluding our afternoon meal, there was a loud knock at the door. It was a neighbor telling us to come quickly, because Reb Shlomo had suffered a collapse. We followed the neighbor in our Shabbos finery to the soccer stadium, one block away from our home.

As we stood near the gate, we heard the feral cry of the crowd erupt in a sudden roar; it was as if the sound was coming from another planet. Then, as we stood and watched, they carried Reb Shlomo out on a stretcher. He was dead. The excitement had been too much for him, and his heart had given out. Can you imagine the shame, my dear son? Can you imagine the humiliation for Reb Shlomo, of being carried out of a soccer stadium on a Shabbos afternoon, that the whole world had to see that this famously pious man would desecrate the Shabbos for the sake of a soccer game? And what was it all about? It was that Reb Shlomo had to win, at all costs. Winning became like a drug without which he could not live.

We all have this urge to win. It is part of human nature. They call it the competitive spirit. It can be used for the good. Chazal say, "*Kinas sofrim tarbeh chachmah.* Competition among scholars increases wisdom." However, it can also destroy a person if it gets out of hand. I once read about a snake charmer who was bitten by his snake and infected with poisonous venom. He had only a few minutes to seek medical attention before the venom would cause a breakdown in his system but, for a full minute, he was silent. Why? Because he did not want to admit to his friends and admirers that he, the famous snake charmer, had lost his contest with the snake.

I remember one Chol Hamoed that your mother and I took the children to the mall. We gave each of you a few dollars and allowed you to buy whatever you wanted. I don't recall exactly what it was that you wanted, but I do remember that your mother was sure it could be found in a certain store, while I was absolutely convinced it would be in a different store. So we split up and went looking. You went with your mother and the other children, and I went by myself. Sure enough, my store did not carry the item. I went back to tell your mother, and she greeted me with an excited, "We found it. It was here just as I said. I was right!"

Believe it or not, at that moment I felt that my pride was hurt. It was as if we were two teams, and I had lost. For a brief moment, I was upset, and over what? A completely meaningless issue, but I wanted to win! Fortunately, I came to my senses immediately. I smiled with pleasure and joined my beautiful family for the continuation of a glorious day. Nevertheless the beast had raised his head, and I knew the feeling of the desperate need to win.

Why do I tell you all this, my son? Because this terrible urge to win can destroy a person's happiness. It can even lead to tragedy, as it did with Reb Shlomo in Buenos Aires. You must not allow it to find its way into your marriage, because it can cause irreparable damage.

Always remember that you and your wife are not competitors. You are one and the same person! Never compete with her. Never allow yourself to feel the urge to win against her, for if you do, both of you will be the losers.

~

My dear son,

I want to go a little deeper into the issue of arguing with your wife. As I wrote to you last time, you should certainly not seek to win the argument just for the sake of winning. Even if you are convinced you are right, it is not always important to convince your wife, as well. Unless the issue is of critical importance, there will be no harm done in leaving the argument unresolved. It is probably much healthier that way.

However, hard you try never to overstep the boundaries of perfect cordiality, there is a remote possibility that sometimes there may be heated arguments and sometimes even, Heaven protect us, sharp words may be exchanged. If the relationship is strong and the occurrences are rare, husband and wife may be able to get past such eruptions, but what about the children? How will they deal with the spectacle of fighting parents?

When I was a young boy in Argentina, as you well know, mine was one of the few observant families. I attended public school, and most of my friends were not as observant as we were. Understandably, I lived with more restrictions and prohibitions than they did. I could not do many of the things they did, nor go to many of the places they frequented.

How then do you think I reacted? Was I angry? Resentful? Not at all! You see, my home was a wonderful place, a real Garden of Eden. My father and mother never said a single harsh word to each other. They respected and cherished each other and were ever so sensitive to the feelings of the children. There was such intimacy and closeness among all of us, and we were so happy. My home was an island of peace, serenity and harmony, and I knew it. It was worth all the restrictions and prohibitions. Why would I want to give up my place in such a precious Jewish environment for a little more fun with my friends? It was out of the question.

Unfortunately, it can also work the opposite way. The positive environment in my home made me strong and secure. A negative environment, however, could be incredibly destructive to an impressionable young child.

A young man with whom I was quite close called me on the day of his wedding. He was very happy, and we spoke about the goals of building a new Jewish home. In the course of the conversation, he mentioned to me that his parents had very often argued in his presence, and then he suddenly began to cry. For many long minutes, he just kept crying. I simply could not get him to stop.

What had caused this emotional outburst? I think it was the pent up fear, anger and resentment that he had suppressed all these years. An orphan is sad, but he cries and gives vent to his emotions, but a child who sees his parents fighting becomes completely disoriented. He does not understand what is going on. Do his parents hate each other? Do they love him? Is the home falling apart? — and so many more painful questions that they do not allow themselves to express. Everything is kept inside, suppressed, pent up, ready to explode.

On the day of his wedding, as he was speaking to me on the telephone, my young friend was overcome by the emotion of the moment, and the wellsprings of his suppressed emotions opened up and spewed out their long festering contents. He cried inconsolably as he shed all those tears that he had stored up and locked away over the years.

The wounds are deep, sometimes so deep that they can never heal properly. Believe me, if the children would burst into tears when their parents fought in their presence, it would never happen again. Which parents want to inflict such deep wounds on their children? Most of the time, however, the children are too hurt and confused to cry. Instead, they maintain a stony silence, while inside there are volcanoes erupting in their hearts. Who knows how they will act out? They could become problem children with behavior problems. They could become withdrawn. Their schoolwork and social relationships could suffer — but this much I can tell you. It is almost impossible that there should be no damage.

Remember, you must never allow the children see you bicker or fight. Even if you think it is not a big thing, your children will see it as a big thing. I know that all this is not in your nature, and that your home is a true haven of peace, but I feel obligated to say this anyway. Forgive me, if it is inappropriate.

— 15 —

Listen Carefully

My dear son,

Let me tell you about a *shidduch* with which I was involved. The young couple met three times. They liked and admired each other, but something was wrong. After the third time, they decided not to continue. A friend of the girl called me and asked if I could try to salvage the budding relationship. After making some inquiries, I discovered that the conversations during their meetings were stiff and formal.

How could I get it across to the young man that he had to allow the conversation to flow more naturally? Since he was a *lamdan*, I illustrated my point with a *Targum Onkelos*. As already mentioned, the Torah tells us that when Yosef's brothers came to Egypt and met him for the first time, they did not recognize him.

For one thing, they had sold him into slavery, and the last thing they expected was to see him dressed in royal garments sitting on the throne of the viceroy of Egypt. In addition, we are told that "*vayisnaker Yosef*. Yosef made himself a stranger."

How did he do that?

Targum Onkelos says that he thought everything over before he said it. In other words, he spoke in a very formal, measured manner, and this contributed greatly to his disguise. Had he spoken in his natural manner his brothers might have recognized him, but the manner in which he spoke was like a mask behind which he was hiding.

"So you see," I told the young man, "when you speak to her in such a formal way, when you do not let yourself go and speak naturally, it is just as if you are wearing a mask. So this young girl, who likes and admires you, is frustrated because she is sitting with a young man wearing a mask. She doesn't know who you really are!"

The young man understood exactly what I was saying, and I was able to arrange another meeting. The most amazing thing happened. During this very next meeting that I had arranged, they decided to get married. Apparently, the masks were off.

What is my point? I am trying to illustrate to you that there are basically different forms of speech. One is formal and analytical. It deals with an issue in a rational manner, devoid of emotion, and tries to make a point as clearly and intelligently as possible. The other is spontaneous and emotional.

Now, when I describe to you the difference between men and women regarding speech or just about anything else, you must understand that these are not hard and fast rules. There are great variations among men and equally great variations among women, and sometimes the two will overlap. Just keep in mind that I am just giving you a general rule of thumb.

If you read a technical paper, a political speech or any other academic work, and do not know who the author is, chances are you will not be able to determine if it is a man or a woman. Academically, there is no great discernable difference between men and women.

On the other hand, when they speak informally in a natural setting, the differences are often sharp. Men will focus on the point they are making and try to bring it across convincingly. They will not involve their emotions (unless that is the topic they are discussing) or offer extraneous information, but rather keep everything clear, concise and logical.

Women, however, are more likely to express themselves from a broader perspective. They will focus on the setting, the mood and the emotions involved, even though they are not specifically relevant to the point.

For instance, a woman goes to the doctor.

"What is the problem?" he says.

"Well, I was at my brother's wedding," she replies, "and I was talking to a cousin I hadn't seen in ages, and suddenly, I felt a sharp pain in my back."

"I see," says the doctor, and he writes in his notes, "Patient reports sudden sharp back pain."

Now, the doctor does not record the wedding and the reunion with the cousin. All he notes is the sharp pain, the relevant information, but she has told him the whole story. Why? Because in her mind everything is connected — the setting, the emotions, the pain. They are all part of the same experience, just as the chocolate icing is part of the cake.

Even as a man, I once had a similar experience. I was renewing my passport, and the form required that I list all former marriages and divorces. I was incensed. How can they assume so casually that I have a list of marriages and divorces? We are good Jews who hold fast to the Torah. We have higher ideals and values. Divorce for us is not a simple matter. It is a shocking event, a deviation from the norm. There was, however, no space for comments, so all I wrote was "none," the essential relevant information. Sometimes, men are also roused to involve their emotions.

The *Maharal* explains that women are naturally more expressive than men. That is why women will talk about all matters related to the topic, while men will say little more than is necessary to bring out the point. It is very important to a woman that she has the opportunity and space to express herself, especially with her husband. The Chazon Ish writes in a letter that a woman needs to converse freely and easily with her husband in order to feel comfortable in the relationship.

So you see, my son, you have to understand this aspect of the woman's personality and be sensitive to it. You cannot be impatient if she suddenly is off on a seemingly irrelevant tangent while you are conversing. This is her way of expressing everything that is going on in her mind and heart.

When a young man and a young woman meet, before they are *chassan* and *kallah*, the conversations will often go on for a long time. It is an exciting time, a time of discovery, and the young man gladly absorbs all her emotional outpouring, because he is eager to get to know her. This patient attentiveness must continue throughout the marriage.

Sometimes, when a woman is telling her husband about an exciting event that took place, she goes into great detail and spends a long time describing the mood and the emotions. If her husband becomes impatient and irritated, she will feel rushed and uncomfortable. In the future, she may be reluctant to share her experiences with her husband, and the relationship will suffer.

I once heard a cute story about an old man who was seated next to a great *gadol* at a wedding. They did not have much in common, and their conversation was limited to the basics of politeness.

Later, the old man's grandson asked him, "So, did you enjoy sitting next such a *gadol*?"

"It was a great honor, my child," the old man replied, "but it was not much of a pleasure."

It is not enough for your wife to feel honored that she is married to you. That will not make her happy. She also has to have the pleasures of the relationship, the warmth and the intimacy.

She has to feel that she can speak her mind and that you will listen patiently and attentively, that you will be genuinely interested in what she has to say, and that you will care about how she feels about the things that interest her.

It is up to you. Rav Yisrael Salanter says that the main *chessed* a person does is with his wife. Making her happy, giving her pleasure, is a great *chessed*. I would like to add that when you make your wife happy, you are doing a great *chessed* to yourself. You will avoid tension and strife and bring harmony and bliss into your home.

— *16* —

Look at the
Bright Side

My dear son,

When Rav Yosef Dov Soloveitchik, the author of *Beis Halevi*, was very ill, the doctors suggested a new medical procedure. Rav Yosef Dov discussed this option at great length with his son Rav Chaim Soloveitchik, and, together, they arrived at the conclusion that they should try it. Shortly afterward, Rav Yosef Dov passed away.

Rav Chaim was inconsolable, blaming himself for giving bad advice and shortening his father's life. During the *shivah*, he poured out his heart in great detail to all the *rabbanim* who came to offer their condolences. One after the other offered arguments and proofs to demonstrate to him that he had done the right thing, but he was not convinced. With his brilliant mind, he refuted all their arguments and remained in his state of deep dejection.

Finally, one *rav* listened very closely to what he had to say and then remarked, "You are right. You should never have let your father undergo that procedure. You made an obvious mistake."

Rav Chaim was taken aback. He leaned back and mulled over the *rav's* words for a few long minutes. Then he said, "No, I did the right thing."

This story tells us a lot about human nature. You see, there were positive and negative aspects to this medical treatment. In his intense emotional turmoil after his father's passing, Rav Chaim reevaluated his decision and was unable to focus on anything but the drawbacks of the procedure. Others pointing out the positive aspects of the procedure did not help. Overcome by guilt, he could not accept what they were saying, and he used his brilliance to refute their arguments. However, when the last *rav* agreed with him and told him bluntly that he had made a mistake, Rav Chaim felt compelled to review the entire picture, and he arrived at the same conclusion he had before. They had done the right thing.

The issue of focus plays a very important role in a marriage. When a young man first gets to know his prospective wife, he sees all her strengths and weaknesses. Nonetheless, he is so enamored of her qualities that he accepts her weaknesses in stride. He sees her as the wellspring of his life, and all her little faults pale in comparison. After all, she is only human, and all humans have some weakness. That is the wonder of being human.

However, in the course of married life, the husband may take offense at something she has done, and he will suddenly focus on her weakness, not as the normal state of being human, but rather as the overriding aspect of her identity. All of a sudden, she is no longer the wellspring of his life, but a hopeless mass of weaknesses, a dead end. This is a formula for disaster.

What is the solution?

When Moshe came back to Egypt he found that the Jewish people were too overwhelmed with their hard labors to listen to his message. He then asked Hashem (*Shemos* 6:12), "If they don't listen to me, how can Pharaoh be expected to listen to me?" Hashem sent him back to the Jewish people. The *Zohar* explains that Hashem told him to be gentle with the people, to remember that they are of royal descent, that they were faithful to their customs and that they did not assimilate with the gentiles.

Hashem was telling Moshe not to focus on their temporary distraction, but on their great merits. They may appear like slaves, but they are actually royalty. They are people who held fast to their cherished traditions and did not assimilate, even under the most trying conditions. Moshe, focus on their positive qualities, Hashem was saying, and they will eventually listen to you.

Let me give you an example of focus. We were once invited to a *sheva berachos* in a bungalow colony in the Catskill Mountains. You know we are not fancy people, but we found the bungalow appalling. The rooms were dank and musty, the beds were lumpy and we were constantly fending off insects. Then again, there are thousands of people who just love the country and cannot wait for the summer, when they can go to the bungalows (this was before they started building beautiful second homes up there). It's a funny thing, isn't it? Why do they love it, while we couldn't stand it?

The difference is focus. They were going to the bungalows because they wanted the fresh mountain air, the wide open spaces, the recreational activities and the vacation environment. The discomforts of the bungalows compared to their year-round homes were, therefore, minor inconveniences to them. We, however, had come for a *sheva berachos*, not for the benefits of the great outdoors and, therefore, the poor living conditions bothered us more.

My son, always focus on your wife's wonderful qualities. The benefits she brings to you are infinitely greater than any weaknesses she may have. Compared to what she brings you, they are minor inconveniences, and they should never cloud the beauty of your relationship.

If there was ever a person in the history of the world who could be justified for having a grievance against his wife, it was Adam *HaRishon.* This man could have reached perfection. He could have lived forever in the Garden of Eden, but his wife cajoled him into eating from the *Eitz HaDaas,* the Tree of Knowledge, and — poof! — it was all gone. He was banished from the Garden of Eden. He lost his eternity, and even during his life on this earth, he was condemned to earn his livelihood by the sweat of his brow.

Surely you would expect that this marriage would suffer, wouldn't you? Nevertheless, look what happens right after this disaster with the Tree of Knowledge. For a brief moment he blames his wife for his actions, but Hashem considers this an ungrateful response. Then Adam gives his wife the name Chavah to signify that she is the *eim kol chai,* the mother of all the living. According to the commentators in the Midrash, Adam thereby acknowledged that *"lechiyus nitnah velo letzaar,* she is there to provide life, not suffering." What an extraordinary response! Even after all the trouble she had caused him, Adam considered Chavah the embodiment of life, a precious gift from the A-mighty!

The Gemara in *Yevamos* (63a) tells us that Rav and Rav Chiya both had difficult wives. Rav was always patient with her; regardless of what she did to upset him, he remained an affectionate husband. Rav Chiya, however, went one step beyond. He brought her gifts all the time.

Rav was puzzled. "Why do you bring her gifts?" he asked. "Doesn't she make life difficult for you?"

This was a serious question, not an attempt to sow discord between Rav Chiya and his wife. Rav wanted to know how it was possible to bring gifts to a difficult wife without being hypocritical. How was it possible to be sincere?

"You know how?" Rav Chiya replied. "Because I appreciate that she raises my children and keeps me from sinning. I focus on merits, which are enormous, and all the rest is not important. The difficulties are only trivialities. All in all, she is a wonderful wife, and I am glad to bring her gifts."

Every husband should listen carefully to these words. His wife brings up his children and prevents him from sinning. These are enormous benefits that every wife has. In addition, most wives have numerous beautiful qualities to delight the hearts of their husbands. If only the husbands would focus on these benefits, all the little faults and weaknesses would become relatively insignificant.

My dear son,

A final thought occurred to me on this subject.

One time I was riding in a car with a few *bachurim*. The driver turned on the radio to the news station to hear the traffic report, but first there was a brief report about the prospects of the President of the United States being impeached. One of the *bachurim* in the car was a big *masmid* who generally paid no attention to politics. The thirty-second report apparently caught his attention. He looked up, thought for a moment and pronounced, "They will never impeach the President."

I looked at him in amazement. How could this *bachur*, who had no knowledge about politics, hear a thirty-second report on an unfamiliar subject and reach such a definitive conclusion after barely five seconds more of consideration?

Such a person, it occurred to me, could bring this kind of instant judgment to a marriage and cause a great deal of damage.

This is an important lesson for all of us. Never rush to judgment in a marriage. The obligation to be *dan lekaf zchus*, to give the benefit of the doubt, extends to a wife as well, perhaps even more so than anyone else. Something that appears at first glance to be a misdeed may not be one at all. If, instead of flying off the handle, you take your time, ask a few questions and think it through, you may discover that she is really perfectly innocent, and spare both of you a lot of heartache.

If it should ever turn out that she did something she perhaps should not have done, I will remind you again to look at the bright side. Consider all the wonderful benefits she brings into your life, and everything else will pale by comparison.

— *17* —

Pure
Cholesterol

My dear son,

When I was a boy in Argentina, there was a man in our neighborhood who ate a lot of meat. That's right, every day he would have steaks for lunch and steaks for supper. There are great cattle ranches in Argentina, so meat is plentiful and cheap. This man took advantage of the situation, and there was never a shortage of meat on his table. People used to make jokes about it, but he would tell them that his protein-rich diet made him strong and healthy, and that he really was a very strong man.

As you know, after I moved to Lakewood, I visited my parents in Argentina at least once every year. On one of my early visits, I noticed that this man was not in his usual place at *shul.*

I asked my father about him. "He is like part of the furniture," I said. "When he is not there, you notice it. Did he go on vacation?"

"I'm afraid not," said my father. "He had a pretty serious heart attack a few months ago."

I was shocked. "A heart attack! He can't be more than forty or forty-five years old! How is he? Can I go visit him?"

"Well, not really. You see, he was gone by the time they got to the hospital."

"But I don't understand," I said. "He was so strong and vigorous. Who would have expected a heart attack?"

"He was strong and vigorous, but the doctors said that he was also full of cholesterol, from all the red meat he used to eat. The cholesterol clogged his arteries and just about blocked the blood flow to his heart. He was a walking time bomb."

I learned an important lesson that day. Things may appear good and beneficial on the surface, but they may be full of poison underneath. Keep this lesson in mind, my son, and you will save yourself a lot of heartache.

Specifically, I want to talk to you about a new and very disturbing development in our community, a change that can easily be traced back to the gentile societies in which we live.

You know, it used to be, in the olden days, that people were very restricted in their time and movements. They worked long and hard and, when they went home, they basically stayed put. However, times have changed. People do not work as hard physically. They make more money, and they are very mobile. You want to go somewhere, you jump into the car, and zoom, you are on your way.

As a result, we now have a new thing called leisure. Married couples are always looking to take a break and be entertained and stimulated. They go to restaurants and concerts and who knows what else. In addition, in order to make the evenings more exciting, they usually arrange to go with other couples. This is what goes on among the gentiles and, more and more, unfortunately, in our own circles.

These outings, my son, are pure cholesterol. Sure, the atmosphere is light, the conversation is pleasant and, afterwards, they feel they have had a nice break from the stress of their everyday work load. They feel more relaxed and better able to deal with the children. They tell themselves that they have filled up on protein and made themselves healthier and stronger by enjoying a pleasant evening out with friends. What they do not realize, however, is that they have also filled themselves up with pure cholesterol; that they have clogged the arteries of their relationship and put their marriage at risk of a massive congestive failure leading to divorce.

Yes, divorce. Are you surprised? How can an innocent evening out lead to divorce? Believe me, it can lead to severe strains in the marriage and even divorce. Let me explain.

In our times, we've seen a tremendous change in the family, in the gentile societies in which we live. Divorce used to be a rarity, a scandal, something to talk about in whispers, but not any more. There have been drastic changes in lifestyle, people have a more cavalier attitude toward life, and the sanctity of marriage and the family have been seriously degraded. It is no longer a big deal to get divorced, and the divorce rates have skyrocketed. More than half the first marriages in the United States today end in divorce.

The situation in our community is not quite as bad, but we cannot completely escape the influences of contemporary culture. Divorce is still the exception rather than the rule, but it is becoming more and more common. We have to recognize that the changes in lifestyle driving the high divorce rate are penetrating our community, and if we want to survive as Hashem's "holy nation," we have to resist with all our might.

In my opinion, a major cause of marital discord in our community is couples socializing with each other. When couples get together, the women particularly present themselves at their very best. They dress beautifully and are carefully made up. They smile and sparkle. The atmosphere and the ambience also add to the effect. Of course, it is all an illusion — not real life. Nonetheless, a husband seeing another woman in that type of setting and presentation is likely to have her image implanted in his mind as an ideal kind of woman. Then he measures his own wife against this image in his mind, this illusion, and his wife may fall short. He forgets all the wonderful qualities his wife possesses and how devoted she is to him. All he sees are her perceived shortcomings, and he becomes angry with her. He resents her for not measuring up to his illusions. The relationship becomes poisoned with the pure cholesterol he has ingested, and who know where this path will lead? Perhaps even to divorce.

There is a Gemara (*Temurah* 16a) that speaks about a woman named Achsa. Why, asks the Gemara, was she called Achsa? It was because everyone who saw her would get angry with his own wife. Rashi explains that because Achsa was so beautiful it made anyone who looked at her grow angry with his own wife. If you see that just looking at a beautiful strange woman can cause discord in a marriage, you can imagine how much damage sitting in a restaurant with a woman other than your wife can cause.

You know, there is a *mitzvah* in the Torah to devote a lot of time to your wife during the *shanah rishonah*, the first year of your marriage. If everyone else goes out to war, you have to stay behind and spend time with your wife. What's the purpose of this *mitzvah*? You would think that it is to give the young couple time to build and deepen their relationship, so that it will remain strong for the rest of their lives. Well, not quite.

The *Chinuch* writes that the purpose is to "accustom himself to her, to focus his desire on her, to absorb her image and everything she does into his heart, to the point that it becomes second nature to him that the actions and affairs of any other woman will be alien to him. Since a person wants and loves that with which he is familiar, in this way, a person will stay far away from strange women, and his thoughts will concentrate on the woman who is suitable to him . . ."

You see, it is not to deepen the bond between them, although this is certainly very important, but to wipe away from his mind all thoughts of other women, so that only his wife will fill his world. Now tell me, does socializing with other couples fit in with such goals? I think not.

Pure cholesterol.

My dear son,

It appears to me that the dangers of socializing with other couples are greater for the husband than for the wife, since the wife is more likely to be completely wrapped up in her husband and devoted to him. Therefore, my son, if the issue of going out together with other couples comes up, the burden of avoiding this dose of cholesterol lies mainly on your shoulders.

If she should ever express a preference for this type of socializing, it is up to you to explain to her that this is not a good idea. You could point out to her that the meetings that led up to your engagement were all just the two of you with no one else present — and look how excellent those times were. They convinced you to get married to each other! Now, too, you should focus only on each other when you decide to take a break from your daily routine. Just as private times brought you together, private times together will enrich your relationship.

In addition, the business of living demands so much of your time and attention that sometimes you do not have the opportunity to sit down and talk to each other, so, if you need a break, spend the time with just the two of you together. It is safer and more meaningful.

Your wife is a wise person. I'm sure she will understand your concerns and agree with you wholeheartedly.

You know, every summer we hear of tragedies that occur in the mountains, when young drivers are involved in traffic accidents. Hatzalah begs parents not to allow their young and inexperienced sons and daughters to drive in the mountains, but it does not seem to help.

Why is this so? Don't parents care about the safety of their children?

Of course they do, but they allow themselves to give in to delusion. The pressure from the children is great, so they tell themselves that their children are different, that they are more mature and responsible and that everything will be fine. Well, all too often everything does not turn out fine, but by then it is too late. All they have left is guilt.

It is the same with couples socializing. The pressure to do it is sometimes quite great, and people can delude themselves that somehow they are different, that it will not harm their marriages. They are just deluding themselves. High cholesterol foods may not necessarily give a massive heart attack to everyone that ingests it, but clogging the arteries with cholesterol is unhealthy for anyone's heart.

My dear son,

These days, people are building summer homes in the mountains that are nicer than anything in the city. Well, it was not so long ago that everyone was living in bungalows. Remember those? Tiny kitchens. Lumpy beds. Fans in the windows. Mosquitoes everywhere — and all for the benefit of the mountain air. All right, I won't argue with that. Fresh air, sunshine and wide open spaces are important, especially for the children.

I want to ask you a question. If everyone in the colony had a nice home and there was only one decrepit old bungalow of the type that used to be so popular, would anyone have taken it? I don't think so. No one would live under such conditions, unless everyone else was doing it as well.

The *Mesillas Yesharim* writes that *kavod*, the pursuit of honor and status, leads a person to compete with other people in his standard of living. Otherwise, he would be content with the simplest necessities of life. He would not need such a large, fancy house. He would not need such fine, expensive clothes. He would not need such exotic gourmet foods. His needs would be simple, and he would be happy. However, since he has to show the people around him that he is important, he devotes all his energies to living on the highest standard possible. The professional economists call this conspicuous consumption.

In the gentile world, this type of conspicuous consumption extends to the wives, as well. Men look for a wife who will impress their friends and neighbors. They seek to show her off as a trophy, as if to say, "Look what I was able to get." She is like a fancy car. Achashverosh called for Vashti to come and show off her beauty to his drinking partners, and when she refused to be displayed like a trophy, he got upset and had her executed.

Understand, my son, one of the main reasons that they go out as couples in the gentile world is to show off their wives and compete over who has the best acquisition.

This is not our way. When Eisav met Yaakov on the road returning from Paddan Aram, the Torah tells us that he "looked up and saw the women and the children, and he asked, 'Who are these of yours?'" He asked about the women and the children. But what did Yaakov say? "These are the children the Lord has granted to your servant." He makes no mention of the women. Eisav wants to talk about the comparative qualities of the women, but Yaakov does not put his wives on display. He does not discuss them with Eisav. He only spoke about his children.

When a Jewish man is focused inward on the holy temple of his home, he sees his wife in all her grace and glory. He fully appreciates each one of her stellar qualities, and he treats her with love and devotion. Here, too, I believe we could say, "*Eizehu ashir hasameiach bechelko.* Who is truly wealthy? The one who is happy with what he has."

∽

My dear son,

You have such a beautiful home and family that I really do not want to dwell too long on the topic of marital discord and divorce. However, I feel I must address it a little bit, because divorce is such a horrible tragedy, especially for the children.

Let me just tell you one story.

A number of years ago, a young man came to ask me for advice about certain marital problems he was having.

"I am kind of embarrassed to tell you what we fight about," he said. "They really are pretty minor issues, you know, like who gets the car and when, who does what around the house, and small things like that, but it's what's behind these things that really gets me down. We are really not getting along. It just takes one tiny little spark to set things off all over again, and then we are at each other's throats as usual."

"I see," I replied. "Of course, you are careful never to fight in front of the children, right?"

"Well, you know how it is. I try my best, and I suppose my wife does, too, but sometimes it just cannot be helped, you know?"

"No, I don't know. There is no excuse for fighting in front of the children. Absolutely never."

The young fellow shrugged. "I guess. Anyway, we have gone beyond that. The situation at home is really unbearable, and it looks like we are headed for divorce. I want to talk to you about it."

"About what?" I asked. "Divorce? Positively out of the question! How could you even think about it?"

This was not exactly what he was expecting to hear from me. "Out of the question?" he spluttered. "Why? It's just not working.

Sometimes, you just come to a parting of the ways, if you know what I mean."

"All I know is that you have children," I said angrily. "How could you contemplate divorce with young children at home? Do you know what divorce would do to them?"

"Yeah, it's a bummer," he said. "But what can I do? I have no choice."

"What do you mean you have no choice? You certainly do have a choice. You can stay together and work it out, for the sake of the children."

"Without meaning any disrespect, Rabbi," he said, "you live in a sheltered yeshivah world. You're not in touch with the real world."

By the way, did you notice that anytime someone tells you they do not mean any disrespect, you can be sure something disrespectful is coming your way? When they tell you they do not mean to be difficult, you can be sure they are going to be difficult. Anyway, on with the story.

"Oh really?" I said. "And what goes on in the real world?"

"Today, people who don't get along don't prolong the agony. If it doesn't work, they get divorced and go their separate ways. It's tough for the children, you can't deny that. But things work out for everyone. The parents usually remarry, and the children end up having two homes, two sets of parents, two birthday parties or bar-mitzvah parties. It's life, that's all, and you go with the flow. It's as simple as one plus one equals two."

What can I say, my son? I just sat there with my mouth agape. The naivete, the callousness, and the utter foolishness. I have to admit that I found myself at a momentary loss for words. What could I say to this fellow that would turn him around? Then I had a flash of inspiration.

"Wait here one minute," I said. "I want to show you something."

I ran down to the basement and rummaged around until I found what I was seeking. It was an old Gemara.

"Here, this is it," I said as I walked back into the room.

The young man looked at the Gemara doubtfully. "You're going to show me a Gemara? Something that says you can't get divorced?"

"Not quite," I said. "You know how boys often doodle on the inside covers of their Gemaras when they're bored or distracted? Well, those doodles are very revealing. Sometimes, you look at some of those scribbles written almost subconsciously, and you get a very good idea at what's going on inside the head."

"Okay," he said. "I'll buy that. I know what you're talking about."

I opened the front cover of the Gemara and showed him what was written there. "Here, read it aloud."

"One home," he read, "plus one home equals no home." Then he gasped as the full import of what he had just read sank in.

"That's right, my young friend," I said. "This Gemara belonged to one of my *talmidim*, a boy from a broken home. One of those lucky enough to have two homes, according to your way of thinking. Well, he didn't quite see it your way. In his mind, he had no home. Are you prepared to do this to your children? Think about it."

Well, I'm glad to tell you that the young man went home and had a long talk with his wife. They agreed that divorce was not an option, and that they would do everything they could to work out their problems.

Last week, this couple made a *bar-mitzvah*, and I made sure to attend. It was such a beautiful sight to behold. The boy was beaming through and through. And the parents? Well, it was pretty obvious that they had recaptured what they had enjoyed with each other in the early days of their marriage.

— *18* —

*Keeping
the Peace*

My dear son,

Two people living together and getting along is not such a simple thing. Look how many books, seminars and classes for about-to-be-weds and for newlyweds there are on the subject. So has everyone figured out how to have perfect peace and harmony at home? Not quite yet. The *Mesillas Yesharim* writes in his Introduction that there are many well-known things that are great mysteries, nonetheless. This is undoubtedly one of them.

Do you know who is the biggest expert on marital bliss? I believe that a husband and wife are the primary experts, regarding their own marriage. Every person is a mass of complexes and biases and he does not turn into an angel overnight just because he gets married. However, if he appreciates the critical importance of his marriage in the grand scheme of his life, and its fragile and delicate nature, he will figure out the best way to bring peace and harmony into his home. As long as he is honest with himself and determined to act in his own best interest, he is his own best expert.

You know, issues come up all the time, points of contention between husband and wife. How do you keep it all in perspective? How do you know where to step back and where to take a stand?

As always, we can take guidance from the our illustrious ancestors who illuminated a path through the darkness for us.

Try to imagine the relationship between Avraham Avinu and his nephew Lot. Avraham was an important chieftain, a man of fabulous wealth and prospects. The A-mighty had promised him the entire land of Canaan as an everlasting heritage. Lot was his nephew, his only close relative, his spiritual disciple, his partner and his heir presumptive. You would think that a young man who was in such a position of favor with his fabulously wealthy uncle would tread carefully so as not to rock the boat. His greatest fear would be offending his uncle and being written out of the will.

That's what you would think, but that's not the way Lot's mind worked. There was a dispute between his shepherds and Avraham's shepherds. Avraham's shepherds always kept their flocks muzzled so that the sheep should not graze in other people's lands. Avraham would never stand for anything that smacked of theft. On the other hand, Lot's shepherds weren't particularly concerned, and they did not bother to muzzle their flocks. After all, they reasoned, the A-mighty had promised all these lands to Avraham, and Lot was his only heir, so everything would be coming to him eventually. Why not get a little head start?

What was the result? A parting of the ways. No more closeness. No more spiritual kinship. No more business partnership. No more inheritance. "You go your way," said Avraham, "and I'll go mine." Lot goes off to join the community of Sodom, the hotbed of evil. He loses just about everything in the destruction of Sodom. He is humiliated by his daughters, and his name remains an everlasting symbol of shame and derision.

Don't you think Lot should have stopped for a minute and considered the future before he allowed things to get to such a point that there was a parting of the ways? Would it have been such a terrible concession to give his shepherds the order to muzzle the flock, in consideration of Avraham's sensibilities? However, he was stubborn about an unimportant issue, and in the long run, it cost him dearly.

Now let's look at Avraham's approach. He makes Lot a generous offer. "You take first pick of the pastureland, and I'll take whatever is left over. If you choose to go to the left, I'll go to the right. If you choose the right, I'll take the left. It's up to you." When it came to financial issues, Avraham was prepared to step back, but when it was a spiritual issue — the question of grazing in other people's land — there could be no compromises. If it meant parting ways with his nephew, then so be it.

Here we have a good set of guidelines for resolving the disputes that arise in a marriage. Before a man gets married, he surely thinks it through and decides that taking this woman as his life partner will bring him eternal benefit. Together, they will build a solid Jewish home that will produce generations of pure and holy children, grandchildren and great-grandchildren. Together, they will build an island of peace and harmony, a Garden of Eden where they could grow and flourish, a place whose walls reverberate with Torah and joyous song, a warm, inviting and hospitable place, where guests could feel comfortable and at home. Wonderful ideals.

Now think: Is it worth putting all of this at risk over a small dispute? From Avraham, we learn that it depends. If the issue is material, step back and concede. There is no sense in taking a stand over a trivial matter and jeopardizing the entire structure. However, if it is a spiritual issue, stand on principle until the matter is resolved. Do not compromise. Be like Avraham, not like Lot.

Most of the time, of course, differences and disputes that arise are not questions of *ruchnius*. Some people would argue that everything is ultimately *ruchnius*, but you know what I mean.

Should we do this or should we do that? Should we buy this or should we buy that? Should we go here or should we go there? The wisest course is to be *mevater*, to give in.

It is not an easy thing, I know. Once you are into a dispute, it's hard to step back and say, "All right, we'll do it your way." However, for the long term health of the marriage, it is the best.

I have a little tip for you, on how to train yourself to yield with good grace. In the early period of your marriage, when everything is still fresh and you are both starry-eyed, it is much easier to yield with grace and not take a stand on minor or even trivial issues. Make it your business to do so whenever the opportunity arises, and it will become second nature to you.

You do not always have to have your way in order to be the man of the house. Sometimes, it takes a big man to step back.

My dear son,

A couple once came to me after a huge argument. She was crying, and he was sitting there like a stone statue. They just sat there without talking. I looked at them and gave them a gentle smile, but it did not do any good. I felt like I was sitting on the North Pole.

"All right," I said. "Let me ask a question, and one of you can answer it. What caused this crisis?"

The husband looked at me and said, "You wouldn't understand."

"Well, maybe I can try," I said. "That's why you're here, isn't it?"

He took a deep breath and said, "She did not polish the silver wine bottle for Shabbos. It was tarnished, like a piece of coal. I was humiliated."

He looked at me defiantly, waiting for me to ridicule his ridiculous statement, but I did not. What would be the point?

Something was going on here. Something more than an unpolished wine bottle.

I turned to his wife and said, "Would you like to comment?"

"It's totally unfair," she sniffled. "I worked so hard making his favorite kugels and baking his favorite cakes, so I didn't get around to the bottle. Is that such a terrible thing? Does that deserve an explosion?"

A reasonable argument, wouldn't you say? Now, her husband was a fine young man, not a wild person by any stretch of the imagination. Something was going on.

"Look," I said, "let's not talk about the bottle for a few minutes. We'll get back to it later. How have things been between you during this past week? Was everything all right? Did you have any fights?"

"No, nothing like that," the young man said.

His wife nodded her agreement.

"Were there any major issues you had to confront during this past week?"

He shook his head.

She gave me a doubtful look. "No, not really," she said.

Not really. Aha. We were onto something.

"Would you like to tell me about it?"

"There's nothing to tell," she said. "We did not have any arguments. Believe me."

"So what did you mean when you said 'not really'?"

She squirmed. "We just were talking about things, you know."

"All right," I said. "Tell me what you were talking about."

She looked uneasy and gave her husband a sidelong glance.

He leaned forward. "We were talking about next Shabbos," he said. "It's my best friend's *aufruf*, and her uncle is making *sheva berachos* for his daughter and invited us. Her whole family is going to this *sheva berachos*, but the *aufruf* is important to me."

"I understand that," she said, "but this *sheva berachos* is extremely important. This is my favorite uncle, my father's only brother. They were in the concentration camps together, and our families are very close. My uncle is a sensitive man and, if we don't come, or if I come by myself, he'll be insulted. So you see, it's not simple."

Her husband nodded. "So we were trying to figure it out, you know, discussing it, you know, very calm and civilized. We were trying to decide what to do so that we would both be happy."

"I see. You disagreed about what should be done?"

"But in a civilized way. Like I told you."

"That's right," she added. "We didn't raise our voices. We didn't say anything out of line. We just talked, like, you know, talked, that's all."

"But there was tension between you, wasn't there?" I asked.

"I guess you could say that," she said.

"I don't know if tension is the word," he said. "Maybe a little stress."

"Let me explain what's going on here. The bottle is not important to either of you — but the next Shabbos is very important. You were not able to work it out, so the volcano was bubbling. Then, when you, young man, saw the tarnished bottle, you couldn't keep it in any more, and it all came out. Would you agree?"

He gave me a sheepish look and nodded. With great relief, the couple apologized to each other for the things they had said in anger and agreed to work out their differences. If they could not, they asked if they could come to me for help.

A happy ending — but these eruptions do not always have a happy ending.

Sometimes, a very small thing can cause such a big conflagration that the damage is irreparable. This is a dangerous pitfall in marriages, but husband and wife do not always recognize what is going on. You have to be on the lookout, my son. You have to examine your feelings and actions and identify your motivations.

The *Rema* in Shulchan Aruch Orach Chaim (250:1) says that it is customary to sharpen the *challah* knife on Erev Shabbos. The

Mishnah Berurah points out that the Sifrei connects this custom to the verse, "And you will know that there is peace in your home." What does a sharp knife have to do with peace?

I think this story I just told you provides the answer. A couple is arguing — or should we say just talking in a calm, civilized manner — about issues and questions that are important to them. For instance, where are we going for Pesach, to your parents or mine? Not easy questions — many ramifications and nuances. Then, they come to the Shabbos table, and he takes the knife to cut the *challah*, and the blade is dull. He saws and saws and nothing happens, so he gets frustrated with his wife for not sharpening the knife, and he lashes out. There goes the peace.

Symbolically, if the knife is sharp, the small obstacles are removed and then there can be peace in the home. As long as the little irritants are avoided, the couple will figure out the answers to the big questions. You see, it is these petty, insignificant annoyances that catch them off guard and set off the explosions.

— 19 —

They're Her Parents

My dear son,

There is a custom in the outside world that people do not get along with their parents-in-law. It is considered only natural for a man not to get along with his father-in-law. As for mothers-in-law? It is usually open warfare. After all, what are the thousands of mother-in-law jokes if not weapons?

However, this is not our way. According to the Torah, a person is obligated to honor and respect his parents-in-law. He has to treat them and speak to them with deference, as if they were his own parents.

I've often wondered why relations with parents-in-law are so much worse in the outside world, and I think it may have a lot to do with the idea of family.

In the outside world, men and women are usually out of the house when they go off to college. More often than not, they are working and living in their own apartments well before they marry. They may have even gone off to live in different cities or states. They can go for months without seeing their parents or speaking on the telephone. Sometimes, they just send home season's greetings cards and, sometimes, not even that. As a result, the family ties are not strong. If, then, there is any tension between them and their parents-in-law, which is not unexpected, what is to hold them back from hostilities?

In our community, the parents are very much involved in our lives as long as they live. I am not saying that it is always like that, but that is the normal situation. When a man gets married, he marries not only a woman but also her family. They will spend Shabbosim, Yamim Tovim and *simchos* together. They will be involved with the children. They will be on the telephone several times a week, if not more often. Therefore, hostilities with the parents-in-law are not a simple thing. Not getting along can wreck your life.

Treat them with respect, and they will respect you too. If there is a rough spot, work it out.

Unfortunately, we are too often influenced by the attitudes of the people among whom we live and, sometimes, a young man may be disrespectful to his parents-in-law because he thinks it is normal and acceptable. It is not.

My son, it pleases me no end to see the wonderful relationship you have with your wife's parents. I see how they look at you with pride, as if you were their own son — which you are! You are married to their daughter, so you are indeed their son. Nonetheless, my son, I feel I should address these points, because they are so important to the success of a marriage.

You know a person has a relationship with parents. Sometimes there are frictions and personality conflicts, but you know they are part of your life, and you work things out. Well, your parents-in-law are your wife's parents, and they are part of her life, and so they are part of your life, as well. You have to make the best of it, even if there are strains.

Who ever suffered more from parents-in-law than Yaakov, from his father-in-law Lavan? From the beginning, Lavan tricked, fooled and robbed him. Finally, Yaakov could take it no more. He took his wives and children and fled into the night. Lavan took his band and chased after them. They had a confrontation and reached an accommodation. Yaakov then told "his brothers" to gather stones and build a monument to the agreement and then he invited "his brothers" to a meal.

Who were "his brothers"? The Ramban says they were Lavan's brothers. Yaakov did not want to address these words directly to his father-in-law, because it would be disrespectful to do so. By not inviting Lavan directly, but rather extending the invitation to his brothers, Yaakov was respectfully implying that Lavan did not even have to be invited — that everything he had belonged to him.

Can you imagine what deference Yaakov showed Lavan, what respect? After everything he had been through, after all the heartache and exploitation for twenty years, Yaakov remembered that Lavan was still his father-in-law, and therefore treated him with respect and honor.

We find the same kind of respect in the way David HaMelech related to Shaul, his father-in-law. Although Shaul repeatedly tried to kill him, David not only refrained from harming Shaul when he had the opportunity, but he spoke to Shaul with warmth and deference. After all, he was his father-in-law.

***

My dear son,

A young man once came to speak to me about the troubles he was having with his parents-in-law. He complained that they were completely unreasonable and intimidating, and he was at a loss about how to deal with them. If he was telling the truth, and I have no reason to believe he was lying, the young man was right! He had been blessed with exceedingly difficult parents-in-law.

"Do you know what my biggest problem is?" he said to me. "My wife!"

I was puzzled. "Your wife? Are you saying that she is also a difficult person?"

"No, not at all," he cried out. "She is sweet and wonderful and kind. She is not at all like her parents. She and they are like day and night. And we get along so well. We are so attuned to each other, like twins that can feel what the other is thinking, even from far away. We are so alike in out thoughts, our feelings, our attitudes, our opinions, our approach to situations and problems. I'm telling you, we are like twins, so you would think that when I have a disagreement with her parents, she would see things as I do. I cannot even understand how she came from such parents, she is so different from them. Right? Well, shock of shocks, she argues the other side and defends the position of her parents. I don't understand how she could do that. I can't understand it."

"Tell me," I said, "do you have children?"

"Yes. A seven-year-old boy and a three-year-old girl."

"Does the boy ever get into a fight with his playmates?"

"Sometimes."

"Do you come to his defense?"

"I suppose."

"Even if you would have acted differently, in his place?"

"Yes, I would. But he's my son!"

"Well, they're her parents! A woman thinks of her parents as the king and queen of her life. In her eyes, they can do no wrong. She does not see their flaws, and her natural response is to come to their defense. Misunderstandings and friction often arise in relations with parents-in-law, and you have to tread carefully. You have to realize that, when you speak against her parents, you are attacking her personally, and you can cause her deep hurt, very easily."

"So, what does that mean?" he said. "That I have to give in to them all the time, even if I disagree?"

"Not at all," I replied. "Yaakov didn't give in to Lavan, but he treated him with respect. If you say a single bad word to or about your parents-in-law, especially in front of your wife, it can be disastrous. Your wife may even agree with your position but, if you step out of line, she will be personally offended. After all, they're her parents! No, my young friend, be smart, be diplomatic, but never ever be disrespectful."

My son, this is the best advice I can give anyone regarding parents-in-law. Even in the worst case scenario, even if there is a lot of disagreement and friction with parents-in-law, if you treat them with honor, if you show them respect, they will respond in kind. In an atmosphere of mutual honor and respect, you would be surprised how many problems can be solved.

$$— 20 —$$

Adversity
and Anger

My dear son,

We were once sitting at the table with a number of guests who were complimenting your mother on the delicious food she served. The conversation continued onto the subject of good food, and one of our guests told us about a wedding he had attended in a new catering hall, just a few weeks earlier. The food, he remarked, was especially delicious; every morsel melted in his mouth, and the taste lingered in his mind long afterward.

"Really?" said another of our guests. "I was also at that wedding, and I actually thought that the food was quite ordinary. In fact, much worse than ordinary. I thought it was plain bad. It tasted like sand."

"We can't be talking about the same wedding," said the first guest. "It is just impossible for anyone to call that food bad. Impossible!"

They argued back and forth but came to no resolution.

It really was a mystery. How could such a thing be, that one person should think the food was just about the best he had ever tasted, and the other should think it had tasted like sand? I tried to solve this mystery.

"Tell me," I said to the second guest, "did you enjoy your company at the table? Was there good conversation?"

"Not bad," he replied. "Most of them were good friends of mine, people I like very much."

"I see. Well, were you feeling well that day? Were you perhaps a little bit under the weather? An upset stomach? A sore throat?"

"No. I felt fine."

"Hmm. Did anyone say anything to you? You know, insult you?"

"Er, no, not really."

"Not really? But a little bit."

"Well, it really was nothing important. When I came to the wedding, I saw the host greeting the guests with embraces and kisses. However, when I came in, he just said a noncommittal hello and told me to find my place card — but I assure you that he did not say anything rude or impolite."

"Aha," I said. I turned to the other guest. "How about you? How did the host greet you?"

"Oh, very warmly," he replied. "He kissed me, thanked me for coming and wished me many blessings for my children."

"Amazing!" I said. "There is the solution to the mystery. You were greeted warmly by the host. You came into the wedding with such a good feeling inside, and you had a wonderful time. And the food was excellent! But you, my friend," I said to the other guest, "you felt the host had given you the cold shoulder. In his defense, perhaps some small crisis had arisen just then and he was too distracted to greet you properly but, be that as it may, you felt slighted, so the food in your mouth tasted like sand."

My son, this story teaches us an important lesson about the deep impact our behavior has on the people around us — particularly our wives and children. The Chazon Ish writes that a woman's greatest pleasure is to feel the approval of her husband. If you are warm and loving to her, you fill her with joy. However, if you are distracted by problems and worries and show her your grumpy side, you will make her unhappy. Her food will taste like sand.

Some people think that their mood depends on outside circumstances. When things go well they are happy but, if they encounter difficulties, they become sad and depressed. There is nothing they can do about it, they think, but they are wrong. The Torah commands us, "*Ivdu es Hashem besimchah.* Serve Hashem with joy." Obviously, it is up to us to feel joy.

A person who is sad, says the Vilna Gaon, is "spiritually crippled." It is like a wound; a lesion. Of course, there are times that a person feels sad and other times that he feels happy, but his general state of mind is in his own control. A person with a positive outlook, with *bitachon* in the Almighty, is habitually happy. As a result, his wife and children are also happy.

My dear son,

It's only a few short years since you got married, so you still remember your days as a *bachur*. I'm sure that sometimes you even look back at those days wistfully. Maybe you didn't appreciate it at the time, but those were carefree days for you. You had no responsibilities to other people, no burdens, and no worries. Your only concerns were your own needs which, besides the need to learn and grow in Torah, were relatively minimal.

Married life is an altogether different story. A young married man has to consider another person — his wife — in everything he does. He has to consider her needs, her attitudes, her moods, her sensibilities. This is not an easy thing. He also has the burden of running a household not only from the financial standpoint but also as the spiritual head of the family. Problems and issues of every sort and color arise all the time. How can you deal with them without becoming discouraged?

As always, the holy Torah provides guidance.

The Midrash relates (*Bereishis Rabbah* 56) that Satan tried to dissuade Avraham from going to the *Akeidah* by telling him that it would take a long time. We see from this that one of the greatest difficulties in dealing with a problem is the perception that it will go on and on. It is only human nature to see problems and situations as endless and, therefore, they are already intolerable. Since we know we will not be able to endure the stress indefinitely, we cannot deal with it even now. They are too emotionally disturbing. They make us nervous.

Most of the time, this perception is wrong. Problems do not last forever. They come and they go, and somehow we manage to survive. Therefore, the first thing to do is to get control of yourself and deal with the problem calmly with your brain, and not with your emotions and nervous system. Analyze the situation and find the solution. Short-circuiting your nerves is not productive. Reassure yourself that the problem is only temporary, that something will work out and you will go on beyond the current problems. It is the truth.

In Buenos Aires — where else — the daughter of my parents' friends married a young medical student. They rented a lovely apartment in a nice quiet neighborhood. The rent was reasonable, and they were able to live comfortably while he was completing his studies. The apartment was not in the Jewish neighborhood, but that was not a great problem. During the week, they took the buses and on Shabbos they would walk to our area in about twenty minutes.

Everything went well for several months. Then, as the end of the gentile year drew, the nice neighborhood became bedlam. All day and all night people danced in the streets celebrating the approach of the New Year. At night, drunks staggered around singing drunken songs. The young couple found themselves barricaded in their apartment at night.

"We have to move," the young wife told her father. "It is impossible to live like that."

"But why?" he replied. "You have a nice apartment at a good rent, and it is not too far away. It should serve you well for a few years, until you are ready to find something larger and better. You're worried about the noise and the drunkenness? I promise you, in another week, it is all over."

So what do you think, my son? The young woman did not realize the problem was only temporary? Of course she did. But her frayed nerves, not her head influenced her thinking. And frayed nerves do not realize that there is a light at the end of just about every dark tunnel.

My dear son,

I must apologize to you for writing about this next subject. I know you have a beautiful marriage, and all this does not really apply to you. Still, I feel it needs to be said, if only so that you can speak about it to others.

We have spoken a number of times about the importance of not reacting to situations with anger. Not only is it not productive, it can seriously damage a marriage. Still, we know that most people will have a flash of anger once in a while, and they may say something that should not have been said.

Tell me, if a Jewish husband gets angry with his wife, will he say to her, "I'm so angry that I feel like shooting you in the head"? Of course not.

The Sages tell us (*Eruvin* 65b), "*Bishloshah devarim adam nikar — bekoso, bekiso, bekaaso.* Three things cause a person to show his true colors — drunkenness, financial pressure and anger." When a degraded person gets drunk, he starts to curse and spew obscenities, but not a fine person. The fine person does not have it in him, so it cannot come out, even when he is drunk. Other things will come out. The same is true of anger. A Jewish man does not think in terms of shooting his wife in the head, so he will not make such a remark, even when he gets angry.

Unfortunately, there is another remark that Jewish men, even those on a high spiritual level, sometimes make to their wives when they get angry. They might say, "I want a divorce. I'm leaving you." This a horrendous thing to say, probably worse than threatening to kill her with a gun. The one who says it shows that the germ of that thought exists in his mind. That is why his anger was able to bring it out into the open.

Such a remark and such an attitude come from a street approach to marriage, which unfortunately influences our own thinking. In the street, people look at marriage as a partnership, an accommodation that supplies some of the needs of both parties to the agreement. What happens if things sour? You dissolve the partnership, and both parties go off on their own. It did not work, so better luck next time. Divorce is unpleasant, but not the end of the world.

That is not our concept of marriage. The Torah views divorce as a disaster, a terrible tragedy. The Gemara says at the end of *Gittin* that the *mizbeyach*, the altar in the *Beis Hamikdash*, sheds tears when a man and woman are divorced. And the children! What about the children? We've talked about that before. True, the Torah provides the option of divorce, but it is the option of last resort, after they move heaven and earth to find a way to reconcile.

There is a big question among the *poskim* if a *get me'ahavah* works. In other words, if a husband and wife divorce, can they still have a loving relationship? Some poskim contend that it cannot be done. Others bring proofs that it can be done, but all agree that it is a difficult question. Why should this be so?

The Chasam Sofer at the end of Gittin writes that the souls of the husband and wife are bound together after marriage just as they were bound together when the Almighty created the man and the woman *du patzufim*, as one body with two face. Husband and wife are inextricably intertwined. They are one soul, one being.

Tell me, if a person has a little heart trouble, does he immediately think, "All right, I'm going to get a heart transplant"? Even without the dangers involved in the operation, would he be so quick to give up a piece of his own self or would he do everything in his power to save his own heart? You don't even have to bother to answer. It is a rhetorical question.

How then can a person blurt out, "I want a divorce; I'm leaving"? Of course, he does not mean it, but the thought, the possibility, is there in his mind. It is an option for him, even if only a very remote one. How can he even harbor such secret thoughts? Doesn't he realize that divorce would rip out his heart, that it would tear his soul in half? And doesn't he realize that making such a remark to his wife could inflict a wound on the marriage that may never be healed?

If he only understood the sublime, divine nature of marriage between a Jewish man and a Jewish woman, if he only appreciated how his marriage defines his entire being, the thought of divorce would be so abhorrent, so alien that it would never enter his mind. As such, if it never enters his mind, you can be sure it will never come out of his mouth.

My dear son,

I hope you have benefitted from reading these letters and that their publication will enable peace and harmony to reign in every Jewish home. I leave you with my heartfelt blessing that you and your wife should forever cherish and respect each other and that your *mikdash me'at* should always be a sanctuary in the *Shechinah*.